For Amilia
in friendship

Till

HEALTH AND WELLNESS TODAY

Published by CelebrityPress®, Orlando, FL.

CelebrityPress® is a registered trademark.

Printed in the United States of America.

ISBN: 9780996688765
LCCN: 2016931804

This publication is designed to provide accurate and authoritative information with regard to the subject matter covered. It is sold with the understanding that the publisher is not engaged in rendering legal, accounting, or other professional advice. If legal advice or other expert assistance is required, the services of a competent professional should be sought. The opinions expressed by the authors in this book are not endorsed by Celebrity Press® and are the sole responsibility of the authors rendering the opinion.

Most CelebrityPress® titles are available at special quantity discounts for bulk purchases for sales promotions, premiums, fundraising, and educational use. Special versions or book excerpts can also be created to fit specific needs.

For more information, please write:
CelebrityPress®
520 N. Orlando Ave, #2
Winter Park, FL 32789
or call 1.877.261.4930

Visit us online at: www.CelebrityPressPublishing.com

HEALTH AND WELLNESS TODAY

YOUR **ULTIMATE** GUIDE TO HEALTH, FITNESS AND NUTRITION

CELEBRITY PRESS®
Winter Park, Florida

CONTENTS

CHAPTER 1

THE WINNING METHOD: WELLNESS THE INTRINSIC WAY

By Sophia Ellis and Dr. John Spencer Ellis 11

CHAPTER 2

TEN KEYS TO HELP YOU TRANSFORM YOUR BODY & SELF-CONFIDENCE — WITH JUST 15-30 MINUTES A DAY!

By Dr. Till Sukopp 19

CHAPTER 3

FRENETIC NO MORE

By Kathryn Crous 29

CHAPTER 4

EXPERIENCES OF GRANDPARENTS LEAVE EPIGENETIC MARKERS ON GRANDCHILDREN'S GENES

By Liz Jelinek, PhD 37

CHAPTER 5

KETTLEBELLS: NO BS FITNESS

By Martine Kerr 47

CHAPTER 6

**BETTER FITNESS IS A LIFESTYLE,
NOT A PHASE: ARE YOU
REACHING YOUR FULL POTENTIAL?**

By Mike Fernandes 57

CHAPTER 7

STRENGTH STARTS WITHIN YOU

By Joe Bellistri 67

CHAPTER 8

**RELEASING THE BRAKES – WHY
'JUST DO IT' THINKING WON'T GET
YOU WHAT YOU WANT**

By Dax Moy 75

CHAPTER 9

**THE MISSION OF MINDSET:
5 STEPS TO TOTAL LIFE AND
BODY TRANSFORMATION**

By Chad Moeller 85

CHAPTER 10

THE FIRST STEP TO FITNESS SUCCESS

By Pat Rigsby 95

CHAPTER 11

GET OFF THE SCALE TO GET RESULTS

By Holly Rigsby 103

CHAPTER 12

13 MINDSET PRINCIPLES
OF A CHAMPION

By Anthony Incollingo 111

CHAPTER 13

REALISM FOR FITNESS

By Dustin Williams 119

CHAPTER 14

HOW TO DESIGN 'GUARANTEED
RESULTS' TRAINING PROGRAMS

By Jon LeTocq 129

CHAPTER 15

HOW TO MAKE FITNESS FUN!
WELL, BETTER THAN FUN...
TRULY REWARDING.

By Niki Davis 141

CHAPTER 16

NUTRITION, EXERCISE
& WEIGHT LOSS

By Rick Streb 149

CHAPTER 1

THE WINNING METHOD: WELLNESS THE INTRINSIC WAY

BY SOPHIA ELLIS AND
DR. JOHN SPENCER ELLIS

Too often across magazine covers, book taglines, and social media promises from dietitians and trainers we see the words "diet" and "program" with arbitrary time frames mixed in with outrageous promises. From all corners of the media, information on what foods to eat, not to eat, how long to sleep, what supplements to take, and how to overcome our most personal mental challenges related to our health and wellbeing are thrown at us at an alarming rate. For a generation of people who has become so used to immediate gratification and anything we want being "just a click away", these empty promises are luring, influencing, and confusing us into circular patterns of trying to achieve wellness and then failing.

We experience a rush when we think we've come across "new" information or a new quick fix to the life-encompassing wellness we've been trying to achieve. We are almost certainly doomed to failure when the diet does not work or we are unable to keep up with a program with our busy schedules. This recurrent failure results in disappointment in ourselves and complete abandonment of our efforts to achieve wellness altogether. We find ourselves at the end of this cycle only to experience the same hope and energy towards some new method when we find it in the vast amount of misleading information surrounding us.

What separates those who look, act, and thrive as if they have achieved the secret to wellness and those who continue on the endlessly misleading cycle? Why do some seem to succeed right off the bat and others struggle for years with trying to get themselves to a point of health and happiness? For how many and for how often can we *really* pull the genetics or lack of information excuse?

For the answer to this, I will not lead you on a wild-goose chase Internet search through articles and advertisements mixed with outdated material the FDA continues to circulate. Those who are successful in achieving wellness are not on diets, programs, methods, and are not living by any one set of rules or philosophy. They don't consider health and fitness *separate* from who they are or an *imposition* on the daily routines of their lives. Instead, health and fitness are an intrinsic part of their daily lives and a fundamental part of the routines they live by. Rules are not rules, but choices that are made. Diet is not a diet but the true understanding of the word. Exercise is not a punishment or dreaded task on a to-do list to prepare for a season or event, but something that is just done as part of a daily routine like brushing your teeth or checking your email.

In fact, living any other way than in line with the goal of health and wellness is living *inauthentically* to who they are for those who have achieved wellness. They have an understanding that to physically and mentally achieve wellness is to live it out for the long term as part of everyday. To choose to not take care of the body through proper nutrition is out of character. To go weeks without physical activity because there's nothing to "be ready for" is not who they are. And most importantly, to think negatively and think they have failed indefinitely if they break from the path to wellness is far from how they choose to think daily. People who have succeeded in making wellness an intrinsic part of their lives have developed daily morning rituals, an understanding that they are not "missing out" on anything by choosing wellness, relieve stress through exercise, use positive language in regards to their lifestyle, and know there is no "end date" for their lifestyle.

Wellness has to start when you start. Unlike a diet or program you decide you're going to "go on" for a period of time, there are no good and bad times to be conscious of your commitment. Those who have achieved wellness start making decisions, which benefit their health as soon as they wake up and not at certain times and not others. Getting into a habitual routine of positive actions is imperative to making wellness an intrinsic part of your life. This routine will vary from person to person, so it is important to customize it to you, your schedule, and your needs. I'm sure you've heard all the tricks of what you should and shouldn't do and eat first thing in the morning to achieve health and fitness. Forget this. Rigid restriction does not equal positive change. What is included in the routine is less important than it is that you have a routine in place. Positive thoughts and actions for physical and mental health, whatever they may be, paired with consistency, is key to intrinsic wellness.

One of the biggest problems for those of us on the negative cycle of disappointment when it comes to trying to achieve wellness is that we often feel like by choosing to make changes in our habits, we are somehow "missing out" on something. If you've ever gone on a diet, you've probably felt like you're missing out on dessert or drinks at a bar. Those around you have more than likely told you you're missing out. To make wellness a lifestyle, you must work to develop the mindset that the option other than wellness is not something greater than your stability and happiness with your health; you are not "missing out" on anything but a detour from where you are happy. Being able to pull back from immediate situations and understand that within the larger picture, breaking away from what will keep you healthy and ultimately happy is where you will actually be "missing out" is essential to making health your lifestyle. Having the understanding that the healthier choice, whatever that may be, is the one that keeps you on the path to stable happiness with both your external and internal self, will melt away any feeling of dissatisfaction or deprivation.

With dictatorial and painfully rigid exercise suggestions being thrown at us from every angle of the Internet, it is difficult for many to find a personal routine, activity, and pace that is both enjoyable and effective for them. People who keep wellness as an intrinsic part of their lives have found an individual way to make exercise a part of their daily routine so that it is not chore-like, but rather something they look *forward* to each day. The more you dislike benefiting your body through physical exercise, the quicker you are to burn out, give up, and fail in your quest for health and balance. Despite what many books, trainers, magazines, and websites will tell you, there is no magic method or routine, no special time of day, no gym or club that can tell you what you like enough to do everyday. This you need to figure out on your own by opening up and trying new things. Paying too much attention to programs and trying to filter through all the misinformation on exercise can actually become a source of stress for those trying to live healthy. Most importantly, moving stress relief from negative things like food or alcohol to exercise is absolutely key.

For many who do not understand living a health-focused lifestyle, the more stress they accumulate the more likely they are to turn from exercise and run to other much more negative stress relievers. However, stress will never go away full. There are things everyday that will cause you stress until the end of your life. How you manage stress is what needs to be effectively changed. There is no better way to ensure that you both look forward to and accomplish exercise every single day than making it the way you *choose* to get rid of stress: the one thing you will experience every single day. This pairing of positive action with the negative action on your body will balance the hormones, thought patterns, and physical results of stress more than you know. As always, realigning your thoughts to seek exercise as relief for stress at its onset is a choice and a vital one in making wellness an intrinsic part of your life. Stress is an intrinsic part of your life regardless of what you do to prevent it. Using exercise to manage it will then intrinsically incorporate exercise into your life in an uplifting and positive way.

One major mental mistake those looking to live healthier lives make is deciding to "go on" a diet, program, routine, etc. Usually, we decide to make these big lifestyle changes to gain a specific result for an event or season. Time-bound goals are not bad; they can be extremely good motivation for beginning to make changes. However, it is when we start to tell ourselves and allow ourselves to think there is an "end date" for our efforts, changes, and different choices that we, without thinking, put ourselves in a position to fail all together. If you are unhappy with the way you currently feel, look, or are taking care of yourself, then any changes you make in the direction of wellness should be permanent. Logically, it makes no sense for us to put effort into moving forward in the direction of our health and happiness only to move back at a set date in the near future. The end date you set to your changes is the date you will allow yourself to detour from your happiness. Why would anyone want temporary satisfaction with his or her condition? Those who have achieved balance and wellness know no end date. They know the choices they make that move them forward to health and happiness have to be for life in order for true wellness to be achieved.

When you start to make changes that are beneficial to you and you start to understand what the choices are that need to be made to better your health, put yourself in the mindset that these choices are for life. These choices are not "for the wedding", "for the reunion", or "for summer". You must develop an understanding that you must be making choices for your happiness and balance consistently to truly achieve the results you're looking for.

The most important determiner of whether or not health and wellness will be an intrinsic part of your life is the language you use internally to yourself everyday. It's cliché and already understood that positive thinking is necessary for positive results but this goes beyond that. What you say to yourself about the choices you are making needs to follow the right semantics in order to truly be living a permanently wellness-focused lifestyle. You are not "on a diet", what you are choosing to eat is your normal diet. You are not "on an exercise routine", you are doing what you do everyday to stay happy and healthy. You are, by no means, "on a health kick", you are choosing to change your lifestyle permanently to achieve mental and physical wellness.

The language you use with yourself should reflect the language you use with others and in external situations as well. Make it clear and understood that the choices you are making are not temporary or part of a plan but are actually a part of who you are as a healthy and balanced person. Language is a strong tool and using it to reinforce the ideas you are moving towards and the changes you are making is an invaluable tool in making wellness an intrinsic part of your life. The more you use positive, permanent, and assuring language with yourself and others, the more the changes will feel natural and the choices will become part of a new routine.

Those who live a health-conscious life do not use language that insinuates any part of it is temporary or a negative aspect of their lives; they speak about it as if it is a significant part of who they have become. Your health has to become a significant part of who you are and the relevant choices, sacrifices, and changes have to reflect that in order for wellness to become an intrinsic part of your life – giving you the permanent balance and happiness many are trying to achieve.

About Sophia

Sophia Ellis is a health and nutrition writer and blogger. Having been a professional writer since her teen years, Sophia currently works in market development and media management for start up companies in Fort Worth, Texas. She studies International Entrepreneurship and Nutrition at Texas Christian University. Sophia's experience as a writing professional covers a range of topics and clients internationally.

You can reach Sophia at: sophiaellisfitness@gmail.com

About John

Dr. John Spencer Ellis - Each week, over one million people enjoy a fitness and personal development program John created. He is the CEO of the National Exercise & Sports Trainers Association, Spencer Institute for Life Coaching, International Triathlon Coaching Association, MMA Conditioning Association and Get America Fit Foundation. He also created Adventure Boot Camp and is the publisher of *Personal Trainer Magazine*. He's a three-time Amazon #1 best-selling author, award-winning filmmaker and Personal Trainer Hall of Fame inductee. John competed in the Ironman triathlon and Brazilian Jiu Jitsu World Championships.

You can reach John at: JohnSpencerEllis.com.

CHAPTER 2

TEN KEYS TO HELP YOU TRANSFORM YOUR BODY & SELF-CONFIDENCE — WITH JUST 15-30 MINUTES A DAY!

BY DR. TILL SUKOPP

Today we have more people dedicated to health, fitness, strength, mobility, well-being and body transformation than ever before. On the other hand, we also have more people that are unhealthy, ill, unfit, unwell, weak, stiff, tired, stressed and unhappy with their body, fitness and well-being than ever before.

Obviously we seem to have a motivational or communication problem. *In this chapter you will learn some key factors and methods that can help you to finally achieve a real and lasting body transformation* (often times joined by a life transformation).

In this information era, we have everything we need to live a healthy and blissful life. But most of us are so stressed and overwhelmed with all the information and things on our to-do lists that we can`t seem to find regular time just to care for ourselves.

Since 2000, I have been a sports and exercise scientist and a fitness professional who is dedicated to find, research and test efficient minimal training, fitness and health programs that produce maximum results. Efficient means a program that yields *maximum results with a minimum expenditure of time and effort.*

I have done studies with specific training and nutrition programs for people who really have less time than others due to their occupation, like executives and medical doctors for example. During this time, I was also travelling half of the week and living in hotels with no or poorly-equipped fitness rooms. I learned very quickly how difficult it can be to stay in shape, fit and healthy when the circumstances are not optimal and you're pressed for time.

Through my studies, my experiences and the experiences of my clients, I have finally discovered that getting and staying fit, strong, lean, pain-free and healthy doesn`t need to be complicated or take much time.

There was not as much need for training for our ancestors as is needed today. Nearly all mammals are physically fit by nature, except modern man. If your training is based on primal movements, integrated in sound training principles and methods, then **you only need 15 to 30 minutes of movement or training per day** – which also includes the warm-up.

Within this time frame you can get and stay mobile, flexible, stable, strong, in shape and have a good endurance. Of course, I recommend spending more time each day for physical activity to become even healthier and to compensate for the unhealthy hours of daily sitting. Everyone can find 15 to 30 minutes, which they can add into their day. One week has 168 hours. Fifteen to thirty minutes a day is only around 3 hrs./wk. **All you need is to dedicate 2% of your time each week to training!**

In the beginning many people need more than half an hour, but they can also benefit dramatically from 15 to 30 minutes of focused physical exercise per day.

My philosophy is based on a minimalistic approach to health and fitness because life has so much more to offer than just training; but if you're unhealthy, stiff, weak, obese or in pain, then it can be very difficult to enjoy being on earth.

KEY #1: TRAINING

For my clients and myself, the easiest way to train is a combination of mobility, bodyweight and kettlebell training. I also like sandbags because they perfectly fill the gaps of the other methods. Yes, ropes, barbells, rings or other suspension devices, rubber bands, jump ropes and clubs are also great and I use them all, but with the 3 to 4 methods or tools mentioned you can get all the fitness, health and shape you will ever need, and you can train nearly everywhere you go.

KEY #2: NUTRITION

It's even more critical that you find an effective nutrition strategy that works for

you and which you can follow most of the time without having to force yourself to stick to it.

You know junk food and an organic farmers' market. Generally, the more often you consume products from the second and drink clear water, the faster you will get your desired results.

KEY #3: MINDSET

Without the right mindset and attitude about your goal and yourself, you won't get long-term results. You have to learn how to respond to stress and obstacles in your life which try to keep you from doing the right things to achieve and maintain your ideal health and body composition. You also need to learn to detect, acknowledge and release the things or brakes which stop you from achieving your goals. This is the most critical factor of all points mentioned.

Most people know all that, or at least they can tell you exactly what they should do to become healthier, leaner and in better shape, but they don't find a way to actually do it.

It seems that they either are not committed enough to achieving their goals or they just don't want it bad enough. It's frustrating to both sides of us.

Many people can be very disciplined for 8 to 16 weeks, but it doesn`t "click" in their head. So that around six months later, it becomes obvious that their initial body transformation turned out to be just a temporary change without lasting results – because most of them get more or less their lost weight back.

Finally, a neuroscientific-based approach to transformational coaching gave me all the answers I was looking for. It taught me why so many people don´t do what they know is good for them and will bring them faster to their goals, and instead, do more of the things that stop them or move them further away from their goals.

I have learned that my clients are not lazy or don`t want it badly enough. Instead there are many obstacles or "brakes" in their life which have priority for them to deal with first, before they can focus on the action steps necessary to achieve their goals.

One of the major obstacles or breaks is that they're simply overwhelmed with stress and all the different things happening to them. To get more clarity in your life about your current situation and the things you want to accomplish, it`s wrong to add even more stuff into your "overflowing and stressed life," like a nutrition plan and a strenuous training program. It causes more threat by your feeling even more overwhelmed, and it leads to more frustration because it seems that you can`t follow the easiest instructions.

KEY #4: REDUCTION, SIMPLICITY, CLARITY

The key to dealing with overwhelm is to work on reducing the things that cause stress, and on getting things done which are more important in the current life situation. This could be various things like getting rid of the clutter in your house or in your thoughts, working on a dispute in your relationship, figuring out and eliminating the triggers for binge eating right after coming home from work, transforming core beliefs that don`t serve you into serving ones and many more, or manage to get more sleep.

Reduction leads to more simplicity. Simplicity leads to more clarity in your life and clarity allows you to focus more on the things that are most important to you. Release your brakes first, then everything else will be much easier and faster.

There are several methods you can use to release your brakes for getting more clarity in your life. In this chapter I will introduce some of them to you.

KEY #5: DEFINE WHAT YOU WANT AND WHY

First, it's absolutely necessary that you clearly define what you want. Write it down. Then take another piece of paper and write it down again in more detail. You can repeat this procedure several times until you get a clear picture about your goal. How will your life in your healthy dream body look and feel like?

This is a difficult task for many people. If you're one of them, then it can be helpful to get clarity about what you don`t want. What do you want to change in your life, body and feelings? Write it down and then write down the opposite of every point you came up with. This is it what you do want. Also get clear about why you want that and what it will mean to you if you have already achieved it. Read your notes every day.

KEY #6: ALIGN WITH YOUR GOAL

The next step can be to write down what you think it will take to achieve those things. Think in action steps and write them down. If you want to improve your body composition then you might want to write down drinking more clear water, eating more vegetables, reducing alcohol consumption, sugar and starchy food (at least on several days in the week), eating enough protein and healthy fats, reducing stress or learning to deal with it in a better way, getting more sleep, getting regular exercise like strength training and interval training or "metabolic conditioning," getting the help of experts like a personal trainer, a nutritionist or a coach, writing down your goals regularly, journaling your nutrition, surrounding yourself more with like-minded people that support you, feeding your mind with positive things by reading books on personal development or listening to audios or whatever you come up with. Write down what an ideal life will look like to achieve your goal as fast as possible.

Finally mark or underline those things that you feel comfortable to start with. Of course, trying to integrate everything from the beginning into your life would be unrealistic. Don`t focus on being perfect but instead on getting better. The goal here is to start to align your thinking and your actions with your goal. There are always ways for improvement, so start with the things you feel comfortable with right now and then add other things when the existing actions have become a habit, not an act of forced discipline. Of course this procedure will take longer than the usual twelve-week body changing programs, but it will lead to a lasting body transformation.

KEY #7: THINK DIFFERENT

Brian Tracy said: "If you want things in your life to change, you gonna have to change things in your life." One of the most important things to change if you want real and lasting (body) transformation is the way you think (about yourself, others and your circumstances in life in general).

Review and transform non-serving beliefs. "I`m fat!" for example, is not a serving belief. How does it make you feel? The reality is that you're not fat, you have fat. That is a big difference, because you also have fingernails but you're not fingernails. How does this feel to you, slightly better? Try this on other beliefs about yourself. Maybe "The Work" of Byron Katie can help you with this.

KEY #8: FEEL BETTER NOW BEFORE
YOU ACHIEVE YOUR GOAL

When you want to transform your body or your life, it's of major importance that you learn to understand that you don`t have to wait for something to become happier. You needn´t lose a decent amount of pounds to feel better or more confident. *Your journey will be much easier when you start to do anything to feel even slightly better every day.* **Start to love yourself and your body more because you're a wonderful, unique person.**

Ask yourself what makes you feel good. Is it reading, going for a walk, exercising, being creative, meditating, listening to music, singing, dancing, having a massage or something else? Think about possibilities to get more of that and start to integrate it into your weekly schedule. Even if it´s short and easy like one to two minutes of deep belly breathing (it`s great to reduce stress in a short time).

KEY #9: BECOMING RESPONSIBLE FOR EVERYTHING HAPPENING TO YOU IN YOUR LIFE (A HARD ONE).

If you don´t take charge for your thoughts and actions, nobody else will do. You have to become aware that you have to take responsibility for everything happening to you in your life. Of course, it's much easier to blame other people, situations, circumstances or something else for your situation, but finally you live in your body, and you're the creator of your body. You feed it (in a serving or non-serving manner), you exercise it (or not), you rest and de-stress it (or not) and you move it to different environments. If you don`t take responsibility, you`ll always be dependent on outside circumstances. You`ll be a slave and you can`t be free. Taking responsibility over your own life is a hard decision, but it puts you back in control. You have caused where you are in life now, so you can also change everything.

KEY #10: BECOME AWARE OF YOUR BEHAVIOR

The concept of "A. I. R." can help you to recognize and transform patterns of behavior. A. I. R. stands for Attention, Intention and Repetition.

Attention: You must become aware about both your non-serving triggers and behaviors and of course also about your serving beliefs and actions. If you don´t pay attention to them, it would be nearly impossible to recognize non-serving habits and to replace them with new serving habits.

Intention: You should be clear about why you want to change and replace a habit. A new habit is established when your brain has built the new neuro-pathways for it, which takes, according to science, about 30 days of daily practice with intention. You must do the new things at a conscious competence level where you have to think about the action. It works better and can be accelerated by adding intense emotion to the new habit you want to establish.

Repetition: Finally, you can only change an old habit if you repeat the actions for the new habit over and over again. The goal is to achieve a state of real transformation where your new serving behaviors have become a part of you, because you do them on an unconscious competence level.

Of course, there are many more things you can do to get the body or feeling you're looking for. My recommendation is to look at this list and start with the factors you feel most comfortable with right now. Don`t try to do all of them at once, it will only lead to frustration and more overwhelm. Work on another item on this list when you feel ready for it. It`s better to move forward slowly and continuously than to sprint and quit.

About Dr. Till

 Dr. Till Sukopp helps his very busy clients to get rid of the fitness confusion and make it simple again. Through teachings of the right principles and methods to release mental brakes, Dr. Till shows clients how to get maximum results for fitness and health in less time and effort.

His mission is to show as many people as possible how simple and efficient fitness training and health can be. He helps his clients to get and stay fit and healthy, so that they can enjoy their life without physical restrictions.

Dr. Till has a degree in sports science from the German Sports University Cologne and received his PhD in Sports Science in the field of Sports Medicine. For several years he has worked in the field of corporate wellness and served as the head coach in a center for orthopedic rehabilitation.

As President and Chief Fitness Officer of the Health Conception GmbH and the Primal Fitness Box in Cologne/Germany, Dr. Till has multiple specialty certifications in the field of fitness and performance training. He serves as a trainer for trainers to helping them to get better in what they do and build their careers.

Since 1996, Dr. Till has been helping clients achieve health, fitness, and sport goals. The author of multiple books and DVDs, he has written articles for the leading fitness and health magazines in Germany and is a sought-after speaker for personal trainer and medical doctor conventions. Dr. Till is called "Germany's Leading Kettlebell Expert" by the media. To date, he has given lectures or seminars in eight countries around the world.

Dr. Till Sukopp offers personal training, group training, online training, online and offline coaching, lectures, workshops, seminars, trainer certifications, articles, books, DVDs, and videos.

Connect with Dr. Till at:
Sukopp@TillSukopp.de
www.TillSukopp.de
www.facebook.com/Dr.TillSukopp

CHAPTER 3

FRENETIC NO MORE

BY KATHRYN CROUS

One night I awoke to a squeezing pain in my chest, a deep sense of foreboding and an inability to breathe. Now I am not certain, but I feel that's not the best combination of things to wake up to. Pain and fear is one thing, but breathing is not optional. As a registered nurse I know that seeing my patients turn blue was never a good thing.

I called 911 and came to the realization that the rest was up to God and the paramedics. After the call, it felt like ages before the ambulance arrived. I remember unlocking the front door to allow the rescue team the ability to come inside should I lose consciousness. I remember feeling the coolness of the leather sofa as I sat down to wait. The pain would not subside and I gave in to inevitability, closed my eyes and leaned back, realizing I had no control. I remember feeling the fragility of time and mortality clearly on the ambulance ride to the hospital. After handing my son's phone number to an officer, I wondered if I would ever get to see either of my sons or my granddaughter again. I think at that moment I realized how little control we have over anything in life. We cannot control other people, events or the weather. Truly the only control we have is how we manage each of the many challenges that life throws at us.

At the time, I was working as a CIO in a frenetic, ego-driven and high-stakes environment. I had moved to the greater New York area only knowing my younger son, Alex. Everyone else was to be a new friend,

29

colleague or complete stranger. It was an unfamiliar, high paced and often angry culture. I had been used to "niceness" of the Midwest. The culture shock was remarkable, and I was working hard to find and define my spot in the life fabric of New York City. I had left my former employer because I was working up to 100 hours per week and that was going to be my future for the coming three years. I don't mind working hard, but I am not a fan of giving up my entire life for work. My colleague and friend, Ty said it best when he told me "This is your job. NOT your life!" Those were words that lead me to finding my CIO role. Although I thought that working fewer hours would improve my work life balance, the hostile environment added a layer of stress I had not experienced before.

How have Americans gotten to the point where working too many hours and not sleeping enough has become a badge of honor? Too often we mortgage our happiness in the present for our future well being. "When I finish high school, I can begin my life" becomes: "When I finish college, I can begin my life" which turns into: "when I get married and settle down, get a house, get a luxury car, the kids get out of diapers" etc., etc., etc. It is endless! And happiness always seems just around the corner yet hopelessly out of reach.

Think back on your memories that are dearest, clearest and most treasured. They are almost assuredly those of times you spent with ones you love. They certainly are not those memories of stressful and long work days followed by nights of not getting enough sleep frenetic day after frenetic night. My most wondrous moments have been simple acts of genuine kindness, attention and pure love. I remember when my children were preschoolers and I would take each of them out for their "special day" with me. Giving them the opportunity to choose what they wanted to do that day empowered them to make decisions and have their voices heard. And I simply cannot forget when my granddaughter spending New Years Eve at the nail salon telling the lady she really doesn't want her fingernails and toenails to match! I wish I had been that confident when I was six.

I remember my son arriving in the ER. On the very long taxi ride from the Upper East Side of Manhattan to the heart hospital on Long Island, he did not know if he would find me dead or alive. It was almost an hour of anticipation and fear of the potential bad news. He is a strong, powerful young man and his hug and hand holding was almost as crushing as the chest pain I had experienced prior to my arrival at the ER. After being discharged from my stay in the emergency department, it was determined that my chest pain and shortness of breath was stress related. I realized there absolutely must be a better lifestyle out there for me, and for many others in my same situation.

To discover what this lifestyle entailed, I combined clinical knowledge with extensive research. I began to realize that we need to make each and every day count, and there are specific and measurable ways we can accomplish this. I ascertained there are seven areas of life that we need to focus on to discover a new way of wellbeing:

1. Physical fitness: The experience of pushing your body and becoming stronger is not the same for everyone. I have had the opportunity to listen to adventure racer Robyn Benincasa speak of the most grueling race conditions she has endured around the world, but I have also watched friends and family members lose weight and get fit by simply walking. It does not have to be someone else's definition of what exercise consists of that one chooses to adopt in their lifestyle. Only you can determine what works best for you based on your current physical status, lifestyle, family commitments and work environment. Walking through the options with an expert can help determine what fits best. A coach can help you move into a fitness program that becomes part of your lifestyle and not just another failed attempt to "exercise" based on someone else's definition of fitness.

2. Emotional wellness: This is best defined as the relationship you have with the person you know best: You! We all have our inner demons that we fight with, our fears, worries, concerns, doubts and regrets. On the flip side we all have successes, positive relationships, family and friends that love us, our sense of inner peace, our sense of purpose and our values, integrity and trust. Keeping the well full with the positive side of this

human dynamic is what leads to emotional wellness. It is the difference between being the victim and being victorious.

3. Community: Humans are social beings. Interaction with others and having a sense of community makes one feel like we are part of something bigger than just ourselves. How we engage that community is unique to each individual. We begin our lives in our family whether it be a natural-born family, chosen family or an adoptive family. It is in those formative years that we learn social norms, interacting, loving, caring and giving. There are those that enjoy being engaged in a community through charitable work, professional environments or activities such as sports or hobbies. All of these contribute to a sense of belonging and add to our individual purpose. The key is to find those activities that make your heart sing and give you joy. Doing something that is expected of you, or that you think others will approve of, eliminates that sense of purpose that is key to making one feel most productive and in tune with one's values.

4. Spirituality: The term "Spirituality" means different things to each and every one of us. Some of us grew up with structured and regular attendance at a church, synagogue, mosque or other physical place of worship. Some find spirituality in communing with nature, practicing meditation, yoga or other ritualistic methodology that transcends the physical life and explores the inner self, the unknown and the external omniscient and omnipresent being that protects and guides us through life. This is what gives one inner peace and the ability to find a greater power to make it through the challenging times we all experience.

5. Rest: Sleep and healthy rest are necessary to keep the human body going. Some people are able to function on a minimal amount of sleep and keep going day after day with little downtime. Others need 8 hours of sleep to function well. Research of late has begun to determine that 7 to 8 hours of sleep are not only important, but vital to keep one's brain functioning optimally. Although some people may be able to

keep functioning with less sleep, eventually they will burn out, begin making poor decisions and not be fully present in their day-to-day lives. Sleep can also be elusive with too many worries and thoughts running through your brain. Finding the sleep hygiene pattern that allows one to move into restful sleep is not always easy and sometimes one needs to find professional help to create that biorhythm.

6. Nutrition: Years of fast food, high calorie and fat-laden diets are a clear path to cardiac arrest or stroke. Finding a way to easily adopt healthy choices into our own lifestyles and cooking is key. Nutrition and food should enhance your wellness and not contribute to disease states including obesity, diabetes and many other chronic health conditions.

7. Purpose: Purpose may be the most important area to explore and define in our lives and personal wellness. Whether that be a professional career, the greater good, a family focus or any other measure that causes one to get out of bed in the morning. Too much stress can be physically and mentally debilitating, but zero stress gives us no reason to get out of bed in the morning. It is the inner drive to deliver love to one's family, professional expertise to your work, or food to the starving in underdeveloped countries. These are the things that keep us going, energized and give meaning to our lives.

Although there are seven separate focus areas that lead to wellness, all of them are intricately intertwined and dependent on one another. Your life is not complete and full without each of those pieces of the fabric interacting and supporting one another. Discovering and committing to the definition of physical fitness that works for you as a lifestyle choice; balancing your own emotional wellness and creating positivity from within; interacting with your community in meaningful ways; discovering what spirituality means for you and how it can help you in your journey; getting enough rest; taking care of and understanding your own nutritional choices and options; and finally, discovering and implementing your own unique purpose in life. These are the seven areas of life that lead to wellness.

I spent too many years trying to please others, trying to prove I was good enough and pursuing the next title in my career. Yes, I made it to the C- Suite, I made lots of money but I was miserable!! When my health began to deteriorate, I knew things had to change. However, the road to change was difficult because I, like many of you, am very competitive and hard-wired to achieve and pursue success daily.

I've come to call this process and road to positive change the Benessere Journey, and focusing on these seven areas of life is the beginning of that Journey.

We all have a limited time on this planet. What if you could make the day-to-day become more meaningful, enjoyable and beautiful while still achieving success in your career? What if you could experience the journey in a more thoughtful, calm and purposeful way, while still having time to take care of your health and the relationships with the ones you love? That is what the Benessere Journey is all about and I'd love for you to come along on it with me.

Let's work together to make it so!

About Kathryn

 Kathryn Crous has spent her entire life and career concerned with healing and healthcare. Growing up in a small town in Canada, Kathryn was exposed to nutrition, wellness, the power of nature, strong faith, family and community bonds from a very early age. Her mother was revolutionary for her time in discovering the power of herbal remedies, vitamins, minerals and other nutritional supplements. Much of what the health community is learning now, Kathryn experienced as part of her knowledge base from her earliest memories.

As a registered nurse, her early career was focused on traditional Western medicine. Kathryn's nursing school education and her years at the bedside built her knowledge base of health, illness, and mental well-being. Kathryn was blessed to have comforted and cared for patients for over 20 years. She witnessed the joys of new life and healing in a hospital setting. However, Kathryn also witnessed people taking their last breaths, families devastated by the loss of their loved ones and the personal grief that came with it. Never more pronounced was this pain than when a 2-month-old twin died in the operating room due to an equipment malfunction. Running past the parents of the infant to retrieve emergency medications in a futile attempt to save the child's life left an indelible mark on her heart that remains to this day.

It was during this tenure that she began her ministry to her constituents in the healthcare environment and made her transition from the clinical world to the executive world. Kathryn has a wealth of knowledge concerning the industry and the changes it has undergone over the past 30 years. The move from illness care to healthcare and wellness has accelerated with a new knowledge base now at everyone's fingertips: the Internet. This timely revolution has included a focus on all aspects of wellness, including nutrition and sleep hygiene as well as physical, mental, spiritual and social well-being. This new industry runs parallel to traditional medicine and embraces alternative healing therapies, and is now her focus and area of expertise.

As a healthcare executive, Kathryn experienced the damaging effects of excessive time at work, the pressures facing executives in corporate

America and the problematic cultural acceptance of working too many hours while sacrificing one's health for work. When the tolls of travel, long hours, poor nutritional options and poor sleep patterns began to impact her own wellness, Kathryn developed a vision for creating a community that is not willing to mortgage their wellness to the current overworked American culture.

Today, she focuses on finding ways to help others improve their quality of life in a work-obsessed society. This passion is what created the Benessere Journey vision that each person's life is valuable and it is important to experience each moment of life to the fullest while balancing both work and wellness.

Kathryn is most proud of being a mother to two sons who have given her great strength and a grandmother to a beautiful granddaughter.

CHAPTER 4

EXPERIENCES OF GRANDPARENTS LEAVE EPIGENETIC MARKERS ON GRANDCHILDREN'S GENES

BY LIZ JELINEK, PhD

EPIGENETICS

Historically scientists believed that an individual's destiny was determined by his or her genes. Epigenetics is a sub-discipline of biology that studies changes in gene expression that do not involve changes in the underlying DNA. The word epigenetics comes from the Greek epi and genetics because epigenetic changes occur outside or above the genome. Permanent epigenetic changes are stored in the epigenome and can be passed to subsequent generations.

Until recently students were taught only that a new embryo is created by the joining of the mother's ovum and a sperm from the male with 50% of the new embryo coming from the mother and 50% from the father. It was understood that each individual has unique DNA that remains fixed for life, with the exception of monozygotic or identical twins, who share the same DNA.

Every cell in the body contains the same DNA, with the master code contained within. This code is the program that directs the developing organism which genes to express when. This binary process controls a series of switches that are turned ON or OFF, directing each cell what it is to become—a heart, a tooth, skin cells, or a brain, etc. Historically, it was believed that the DNA remains fixed throughout the life of the individual.

However, through interaction between the developing organism and the environment the expression of genes can be changed, while the underlying DNA remains the same. Epigenetic changes occur outside or above the code contained within the DNA, and are stored in the epigenome. Whereas DNA determines the genotype, the epigenome determines phenotype. Epigenetic changes can result in dramatically different phenotypes, so that genetically identical twins can look and behave very differently from one another.

People often comment that they are forever changed as the result of a particular event or experience. A traumatic event such as 9/11, wars or forced migrations from the homeland, such as that which is happening today in the Middle East and parts of Africa, tends to result in epigenetic changes with unwanted results, including mental and/or physical stress, disease or other disorders. The good news is that negative effects can be reversed by making positive changes in diet, exercise, and by adding meditation, positive thinking and other changes in surroundings through the use of colors, textures, lighting, music, and so on. On the other hand, positive experiences, sometimes known as peak experiences, can result in the growth of new neuronal pathways in the brain. This enhances the brain's ability to learn and to experience life more fully and in a more positive way.

AGOUTI MICE

One of the earliest researchers in epigenetics, Professor of Radiation Oncology, Dr. Randy Jirtle, was interested in discovering if the Agouti gene, responsible for producing laboratory mice with ravenous appetites, and prone to obesity, diabetes and cancer, could be silenced. Jirtle and a group of his post-doctoral students at Duke University took pairs of fat, yellow lab mice that carried the Agouti gene. Beginning with conception, the mother mice were given methyl-rich diets.

Methyl factors are small chemical markers that act as switches, turning genes ON or OFF, silencing the expression of the Agouti gene. Methyl-rich diets are found in common foods, including onions, garlic, beets, and food supplements rich in folic acid. Folic acid is often given to pregnant women, or women who are planning to get pregnant. Agouti mice generally produce offspring that are identical to the parent mice—fat, obese mice that are susceptible to numerous life-shortening diseases, including diabetes and cancer. However, the addition of the methyl-rich diet fed to these mice, produced offspring that were slim, brown, and virtually immune to the life-shortening diseases that resulted in a radically shortened lives of the parent mice.

DUTCH HUNGER WINTER

One of the most studied periods in history is the Dutch Hunger winter of 1944-1945. A rail strike, a Nazi food embargo, and the coldest winter in history resulted in an extreme food shortage in the still German-occupied territories of Holland's northwest. By November 1944, rations plummeted to 1000 calories a day per person, and by spring food supplies allowed only 500 calories a day. Over 20,000 people died and those who lived suffered terribly.

The Dutch are impeccable record keepers, leaving an already established cohort for future researchers with an abundance of historical data. Research using data from the Hunger Winter and the health histories of individuals who were still in utero in various phases of development during the famine, shows show that prenatal famine is associated with various unpleasant or sometimes life-threatening consequences later in life, including increased risks for heart disease and higher incidences of schizophrenia. A greater prevalence of schizophrenia was also found in the offspring of women who were pregnant during the Chinese famine of the Great Leap Forward in 1959-1960.

STRESS

In the mid-1930s, Hans Selye, MD, PhD, of McGill University in Montreal, Canada was a pioneer and one of the earliest researchers to isolate the existence of the stress response. It was Selye who coined the term stress, long before other physicians considered stress to be an important factor in diagnosing disease in their patient. According to Selye, stress can be anything from prolonged food deprivation, swallowing a foreign substance, a good workout, or a great evening out. Selye suggested stress could be positive or negative, and still impact the individual. Although he was unable to isolate the numerous functions of glucocorticoids, Selye was the first to consider the importance of the environment in the apparent genetic variations he observed. He isolated individual stress responses and also noticed that some responses to stress are culturally-specific—entire communities often respond to a traumatic event in similar ways.

BEHAVIORAL EPIGENETICS

Fifty years later, also at McGill University, Drs. Moshe Szyf and Michael Meaney discovered postnatal inheritance and introduced the new discipline of behavioral epigenetics. They discovered the environment continues to influence genomic expression throughout the lifetime by exploring the influence of behavior of rat pups and their mothers, and that positive life experiences can change the expression of the genes as significantly as trauma can. Rat pups with high-nurturing mothers were better able to handle environmental stressors later in life. Pups with non-nurturing mothers experienced epigenetic changes that resulted in pups that struggled with stressful situations, they startled easily, exhibited high stress behaviors—they grew up to be nervous wrecks!

In later research with human subjects, Szyf and Meaney found that timing is an important factor. If a child's parents experience a major life change like winning the lottery, the effect on genomic expression is greater on a child who is around two years old, than it would be if the child had grown to adulthood when the parents had the same windfall.

With advances in epigenetic research, it was found that the separation of an infant from its biological parent, in particular the mother, causes extreme stress that is accompanied by significant unwanted epigenetic changes that can persist for a lifetime, resulting in increased vulnerability to disorders of mental and/or physical health. The stress is generally so severe that parenting adopted children requires significantly more nurturing to reverse these unwanted epigenetic effects. Although such early stress is not a simple fix, it is possible for individuals who did lose their biological parents at birth can, by implementing the positive lifestyle-changing mentioned earlier, have a definitively positive effect as well.

EPIGENETIC RESPONSES TO TRAUMA

Today scientists emphasize the biological basis for trauma, and suggest that humans share innate responses to perceived threats that are common to animals and birds—fight or flight. Trauma specialists, Drs. Peter Levine and Anngwyn St. Just, suggest there is a third response to threat—to freeze. Animals and birds easily shake off this frozen state, but humans appear to have forgotten how to re-set, resulting in the frozen trauma being stored in the body. Frozen trauma results in epigenetic changes that can continue to impact the individual for his or her entire life, and can also be passed on to offspring for several generations.

PTSD

Dr. Rachel Yehuda is Professor of Psychiatry and Neuroscience at Mount Sinai Hospital in New York City. She is a recognized leader in the field of traumatic stress and Post-traumatic Stress Disorder (PTSD). Her research on cortisol and brain functions has revolutionized the understanding and treatment of PTSD, including the transgenerational transmission of both. In her research with Holocaust survivors, Yehuda discovered that children and grandchildren of Holocaust survivors are impacted as much as their parents, as a result of epigenetic inheritance of the traumas experienced by their parents.

This is made possible because heritable epigenetic markers are stored in the epigenome, creating a biological memory of the experiences suffered by their parents who survived the horrors of the Holocaust. These inherited epigenetic changes, as the result of their parents' traumas, result in increased susceptibility to PTSD, depression, and other mental disorders in the offspring of survivors. Historically, it was assumed that this increased vulnerability to stressors, found in the children of Holocaust survivors, was due to environmental factors such as poor child-rearing practices of traumatized parents. Whereas there could be some truth to the idea that parents who experienced extreme traumas have difficulties raising their own children, today science can demonstrate that the increased vulnerability to stressors found in children of Holocaust survivors is inherited biologically.

In addition, children of Holocaust survivors often have nightmares in which they are being chased, persecuted, or tortured, and they are convinced they are going to be annihilated. These offspring of survivors of extreme traumas are reliving the horrific experiences of their parents or grandparents from WWII, experiences that were passed epigenetically across generations. These offspring of Holocaust survivors have inherited the unresolved unconscious minds of their parents or grandparents.

EPIGENETIC INHERITANCE OF THE EFFECTS OF WAR

Since WWII, it has become increasingly more apparent that veterans tend to exhibit increased vulnerability to PTSD and other mental disorders. Not much has been written about the effects of war on returning soldiers from WWII, except the occasional reference to a phenomenon, known as shell-shock. These veterans were encouraged to remain quiet about their experiences from the war, and although many were able to tough it out, unfortunately not all veterans could. However, by the time veterans of the Vietnam War and the Gulf War returned home, it was an acknowledged fact that many suffered from PTSD, resulting in epigenetic changes that were transmitted to their children and grandchildren, resulting in significantly altered vulnerability to PTSD and other pathologies.

WORLD TRADE CENTER DISASTER

Survivors of the collapsed or damaged buildings as a result of the attacks on the World Trade Center on September 11, 2001, were among those exposed to the majority of the reported injuries, air pollution, and traumatic events. Health outcomes were evaluated from interviews conducted from September 5, 2003, through November 20, 2004, by the World Trade Center Health Registry. It was intended that the Health Registry would continue to monitor the mental and physical health of the more than 70,000 individuals who were impacted by the disaster and enrolled in the Registry for a minimum of 20 years. However, recent reports indicate that funding is about to expire after 15 years, or in 2016. The enrolled subjects were limited to adult survivors of the collapsed buildings, excluding those who were involved in rescue and recovery operations.

More than half of the survivors of the collapsed buildings were caught in dust and debris clouds resulting from the collapse of the twin towers, while the majority experienced traumatizing psychological events. Physical injuries were also common, but few reported injuries requiring extensive medical treatment. However, many experienced serious respiratory problems, serious heartburn and/or acid reflex, or severe headaches. These serious effects resulted in major epigenetic changes that are likely to be transmitted to subsequent generations.

NATURE VS NURTURE

The argument between nature vs nurture has been argued by philosophers and psychologists for hundreds of years, changing as each new theorist became the theorist of the times—known as the zeitgeist of the times. The world's greatest thinkers have regularly disagreed on how behaviors develop and how these behaviors are passed across generations. However, with the widespread and diverse research in the new science of epigenetics, it has become readily apparent that the argument no longer has a basis. Indeed, everything that is passed to future generations has both a behavioral aspect which in turn results in biologic epigenetic heritable changes.

Liz Jelinek, PhD – November 1, 2015

About Liz

Dr. Liz Jelinek is a Personal Health and Wellness Coach, a Business Coach, therapist, speaker, author, and educator. Liz has been a freelance writer for many years, covering a diverse number of topics for a variety of magazines and journals—and was also a theatre critic for local newspapers. Prior to changing career paths from performance to the healing professions, Liz spent many exciting and successful years in the theatre as a Director, Producer and Actor, with additional expertise in costume, makeup, and scenic design.

Liz was an invited panelist at the Western Psychological Association, a Division of the American Psychological Association. She presented at Yale University Conferences, the United States Constellations Conference, as well as the North America Constellations Conference. She has led numerous workshops and classes throughout the Midwest, California, and Canada.

Liz is passionate about everything she does and brings a broad range of knowledge, experience, and enthusiasm to every endeavor. She has traveled extensively around the world, and holds numerous degrees in a variety of subjects that include Psychology, Theatre, Ancient Religions, and Healing Arts of the Egyptians and Greeks. Her doctoral dissertation, *Epigenetics: The Transgenerational Transmission of Ancestral Trauma, Behaviors and Experience*—describes the biology of heritable trauma. Liz is one of the leading experts helping individuals to identify and heal from epigenetically inherited ancestral trauma—especially PTSD.

Dr. Jelinek is Founder and Director of the MIDWEST INSTITUTE FOR SYSTEMIC CONSTELLATIONS, which offers training for facilitators and therapists, and workshops for the public. Systemic Family Constellations, is a phenomenological group process that offers healing through the use of representatives who stand-in for the ancestors, making it possible for client to heal ancestral entanglements and traumas, and live a happy, joyful life—and achieve success, and ultimately peace.

Liz' newest venture, the Institute for Creative Dynamics, will stress Liz' expertise as a personal, business, and wellness coach, offering graduate level Continuing Education Training and Certification for Coaches, Therapists, Social Workers, and Psychologists. She plans weekly and monthly talks and blogs on a variety of topics, as new discoveries are introduced in science, medicine, and business.

In mid-January 2016, Liz was appointed to the Advisory Board of the Oxford Education Group, and hired as Dean of Counseling Services, at the Oxford STEM Charter School, Guam.

Liz is a woman of many talents and tireless energy whose greatest joy is helping others to be the best they can be. With Liz—dreams become reality!

CHAPTER 5

KETTLEBELLS: NO BS FITNESS

BY MARTINE KERR

On a typical sunny Dubai morning, a trio of students arrived for their first of several kettlebell training workshops.

➤ *Exercise newbie and mom of two, Lana, was first. Ready to make fitness a priority but clueless about kettlebells, she wanted to understand how they worked before deciding if swinging metal was such a good idea.*

➤ *Next was Cassie. She'd watched friends benefit from them—fat loss, sculpted muscles, more strength, boosted energy—but was suspicious. She'd seen first-hand how quick downhill it goes when good kettlebells happen to bad users at gyms and on the Internet. Plus, how could kettlebells add to her already solid fitness habit?*

➤ *Finally came former rugby player and avid boot camper Rick. He was super-keen to kick his fitness into high gear around his busy work and family schedule.*

KETTLEBELLS

You know. Or maybe you don't. . . it doesn't make you a bad person. For those still in the dark, imagine a bowling ball. Now add a handle. Behold: the kettlebell! It's as simple as that. Other than it doesn't have finger-holes, is cast iron, comes in various weights and is seriously badass.

Let me tell you a secret: they don't bite and are easier to use than you might think. I've taught hundreds of Lanas, Cassies, and Ricks how to lose fat, get strong, move well and feel fantastic with them.

Why? Because I'm on a mission—to help people BE MORE by living FITTER, and to show them how kettlebells fit in (pun totally intended). And YOU are part of my master plan, so let me:

- Explain what smart kettlebell training can do for you and why the word SMART is key

- Quash nagging myths

- Entice you to give them a chance

Warning: common sense required!

You need some before starting to lift, squat or swing a piece of iron; plus, your doctor's ok to exercise. Don't meet the criteria? Step away from all sharp or blunt objects and move on to the next chapter, for everybody's sake. I won't tell. Otherwise, let me invite you into my community of people who transformed their lives and fitness with smart kettlebell training.

LANA

Fitness: Where do I start?

Remember my newbie? Seems she disliked exercise. A potential problem since fitness had recently become her priority. And with so much confusing and conflicting information, she was nerve-wracked! Who wants to make a wrong choice?

I can't blame anyone for not knowing what to believe. The fitness industry's goal is making money. They want us itching for the newest, latest and greatest answer to our every dream...until the next newest thing comes along. We're overwhelmed by choices, each drenched in persuasive hype.

With fifteen pre-kettlebell years in corporate marketing, I got skilled at detecting bullshit—my own and everyone else's. So it pleases me to share a fitness truth that cuts through my industry's BS:

Fitness isn't complicated when you focus on moving well, functional movement, and consistent action.

Moving well means not trying to stack fitness on top of dysfunction. Bad posture and iffy movement habits feed weaknesses that stall results, make you ache and drain performance. **Functional movement** is training that respects how your body is designed to move and makes you better at it. **Consistent action** relates to getting things done. Goals don't magically happen from good intentions.

WHAT'S A KETTLEBELL?

You know, that badass iron ball with a handle? Turns out that the unique shape and offset center of gravity packs kettlebells with oodles of fat loss, strength, endurance, stability, core and cardio building power.

In your hands, power can be used for good—I call that smart kettlebell training—or for evil—that's exercising (or whatever) with a kettlebell. A world of difference lays between them.

Smart kettlebell training will:

• Melt fat and sculpt muscles

• Improve posture and movement habits

• Reduce aches from ignored or abused muscles

• Get you stronger so you can do more

• Save you time with efficient workouts

• Teach you to lift without stressing your back

• Boost your heart and lung health

Just using a kettlebell (instead of a dumbbell or handbag) while moving will either fall short of these benefits or get you hurt.

Exercising with a kettlebell is NOT the same as smart kettlebell training.

If it looks stupid, it probably is.

KETTLEBELL FUNDAMENTALS

Humans are supremely adaptable—we get good at what we repeatedly do. But there's a downside: by practicing crap, we become really good at being really bad.

That's why we build smart kettlebell training from fundamental principles that respect human movement science, including biomechanics, functional anatomy, kinesiology, and motor learning. They keep us safe, improve our skills and deliver results.

Becoming a black-belt in the basics is about YOU, not the kettlebell. That's why we start our fundamentals without one.

I. Your spine rules.

If you don't know how to stabilize your back during or while resisting movement, it's time you learn. Quality movement puts your spine first. Don't do it? You've upped your chances of fatigue, tightness, aches and pains from over or under used, abused or ignored muscles. Lower back too arched? Tail tucked under? Ribs thrusting upward? Mid back hunched? Text head? Fix it.

II. Brace your core.

Your core is the muscular corset surrounding your spine: armpits down to your pelvis, circling front, sides, and back. Expert core bracers have volume controls to dial in perfect tension for any task. Bracing goes hand-in-hand with spine prioritization.

III. Hinge at the hips.

Your spine shouldn't tag along for every ride your hips want to take. They need to move independently. Good hip hinging keeps your back safe when you lift. Plus, it unlocks leg power. Great news: after learning to use your core to prioritize your spine, hinging is easy.

IV. Pack your shoulders.

Passively hanging your arms from your torso by their soft tissue attachments, especially while holding something heavy, invites shoulder disasters. Learn to retract your upper arm bones into their sockets, depress your shoulders away from your ears, and tuck—not crank—your shoulder blades into opposite back pockets. By the way, learning to move your arms without your ribs tagging along is another life skill to learn.

V. Quality trumps quantity.

I'm not impressed by how many times you can do something badly. Injuries happen when ego kicks quality out the window. MORE is not better—BETTER is better. Stop at technical failure—BEFORE things get ugly.

Don't be scared of learning or re-learning basic principles. They are how the human movement system is supposed to work! They get you the most from kettlebells and boost all of your fitness results, regardless of what you enjoy. Use your new knowledge to decide whose advice you trust—and whose is full of s#@#—whether you hire a trainer, buy a book, take a class, read an article or watch videos. It's how Lana learned to like exercise!

CASSIE

Kettlebells: Are you insane?

Having seen way too many people exercising their stupidity with kettlebells, I wasn't shocked by Cassie's reluctance, nor by myths that plague smart kettlebell training. These idiots are why people are scared of kettlebells! So how do we get rid of knuckleheads and their ridiculous demonstrations? By replacing them with better-trained people. Time to set four misconceptions straight.

1. Kettlebells are dangerous

Kettlebells are NOT dangerous—how YOU move with them (or

dumbbells, suitcases, boxes, kids, etc.) could be. Your habits and lifestyle, and how your body has adapted to them, could be dangerous. Most kettlebell and exercise injuries come from ignoring fundamental principles, being unaware of funky movement patterns, lifestyle adaptations, having unaddressed movement dysfunctions, or plain stupidity. That's exactly why I recommend a coach while you master the basics. They'll see through mere distractions and target linchpin issues to keep you safe, your skills progressing and results coming.

2. You need to be fit to train with them

Hogwash. Kettlebells come in all sorts of weights and training plans for every fitness and experience level. I've had 70+ year-olds learn, as well as teenagers. With only a couple of basic moves, you can progress towards two of the most common fitness goals—feel amazing in your skin and/or rock a pair of jeans. Fitness should improve your life, not just make you good at exercise.

3. They're complicated

No, they aren't. Once you've got the basics, kettlebell training is as simple as using a few exercises. You just need to DO it. I love that it focuses on movements, not muscles; fitness results, not entertainment. Low tech, high concept training at its best.

4. I don't need them, I already train with weights

I would never insist that you NEED them, but I will challenge you to give them an honest go if your exercise routine has fizzled out or isn't delivering the results you want. Many of my students add them to boost their existing programs or sport training. This was the clincher for Cassie. After years of dedicated gym work, kettlebell training changed her body more than anything else—running, classes, gym workouts—in less time and with fewer injuries. This was miles from what the idiots did.

RICK

Let's go!!

Rick couldn't wait to throw around some iron. That was until I dropped the hammer.

You see kettlebell training is like me—disher of tough love. Finding out that his hip hinge (remember the principles?) was a squat was bad enough. But asymmetries that increased his risk of injury, especially given a quirky knee? Those were hard pills for him to swallow. Without awareness that his body was compensating, he couldn't fix problems he didn't know he had. No longer able to hide or cheat, Rick worked his corrective exercises, and within a few weeks, put his improved movements and newly-learned skills towards better fitness.

But being a high-intensity guy and former runner—used to punishing his body to finish every set, go longer, and go harder—he faced another challenge. Learning to feel when things were about to sour so he could stop safely rather than cement old habits. It took some practice with me calling quits at technical failure for him to finally shift his "do or die" mentality. Don't think he wasn't working hard. Focusing on foundational kettlebell techniques—the Swing, Squat, Turkish-Get-Up and Clean & Press, with pushups and planks sprinkled in for good measure—he worked his entire body, his brain, and his mindset. To satisfy his need to feel worked and his love of sweat, I just had him do more sets of quality movement. That's it: training sessions designed for effect, not entertainment.

Funny thing is that Rick's brain hit a roadblock when it came time for more advanced swing variations. So what! You don't need a catalogue of exercises for training to be effective. Even after knee surgery and rehab, we returned to the basics with an added focus on bodyweight stability—corrective exercises that had him sweating in no time.

YOU

Are you in?

So you see, starting with the fundamental principles puts the SMART into kettlebell training. Well, that plus learning from a qualified coach. It also makes training accessible to anyone meeting three criteria: have a body, should move well, have common sense. Learning how to use them for good is the best way to safe and effective results. Doing the work determines the results you get and how fast you get them.

They aren't dangerous or complicated and even the most unfit can learn. Advanced skills and heavier weights come when you are ready.

Can you relate to my superstars? Maybe you're a tad curious on how smart kettlebells training can help YOU live fitter—burn fat, get stronger, move better, feel awesome? At the very least, I hope you aren't scared of them. Or blame them for idiots exercising their stupidity.

Since you bought this book, I assume that you care about your fitness. Give kettlebells a try. For me, it was love at first swing...and I've never looked back.

About Martine

Martine wants to live in a world where whining doesn't exist, exercise is everyone's habit, bad repetitions are shunned, stupid people don't use kettlebells, no one hires idiot trainers, and chocolate is a vegetable.

As a sought-after kettlebell training expert and StrongFirst Team Leader, she's been featured on markdegrasse.com / rdellatraining.com / kettlebellworkouts.com / Women's Health & Fitness Middle East / Time Out Dubai / and fitnesslink.me.

With some 20 years as a fitness instructor, Martine's training career took a post-MBA staycation when finance and marketing interests called. Her son's arrival in 2006 came with a realization: she wouldn't leave the world a better place by making people richer. Aha—she could by helping people live fitter so they could be more!

Feeling the fear but doing it anyway, she swapped Armani for Lululemon and KULT Fitness was born (originally known as kerrFIT).

Another life changing moment happened in 2007: she discovered that hardstyle kettlebell training was her perfect answer to residual pregnancy weight and sleepy butt syndrome. It was love at first swing. She sought out the world's leading kettlebell fitness expert, Pavel Tsatsouline, which led to her RKC and SFG certifications and eventually to her appointment to the StrongFirst leadership team. Always motivated to bring the best to her students, she pursues knowledge like chocolate, with a few more certifications along the way and since.

When she's not sprinkling her kettlebell and movement wisdom to get people fit, traveling the world to mentor new instructors and creating training videos for her popular Instagram account, you can find her watching indecent amounts of Masterchef, testing newly discovered iOS video apps and optimistically checking her Dubai doorstep for Amazon.com deliveries.

Her first online student training resource—Training with KULT —goes live in April 2016, quickly followed by THE NEW KETTLEBELL INSTRUCTOR TOOLKIT.

Discover how to join her online training membership or subscribe to her technique video series, where she's teaching next, and how to kick start your kettlebell instructor career at: www.kultfitness.com.

StrongFirst TL, StrongFirst Bodyweight Instructor (SFB), CK-FMS, Yoga Tune Up®, Flexible Steel Specialist Instructor, Ground Force Method National Instructor, CrossFit Level 1 Trainer, CrossFit Kettlebell Trainer, CrossFit Mobility Trainer, TPI Certified Level 1, TRX, RKC, ACE Group Fitness, REPS Level 2, MBA

Find three easy-at-home training samples at: www.kultfitness.com/healthandwellnesstoday with special tutorials on how to do each movement safely.

Connect with her:
Instagram: @kult_fitness
Facebook: Kult Fitness
Twitter: @kultfitness

CHAPTER 6

BETTER FITNESS IS A LIFESTYLE, NOT A PHASE:
ARE YOU REACHING YOUR FULL POTENTIAL?

BY MIKE FERNANDES
Strength and Conditioning Specialist
and Certified Personal Trainer

We are all different ... So why are we all doing the same thing to become better physically?

I loved sports growing up and still do—especially baseball. In order to be competitive in what I loved, I needed to pay attention to training—both on the field and in the weight room. What I didn't anticipate was how much it would become a part of my life. From both my successes and mistakes in my own training, along with those of others, I learned how crucial it is to approach each person differently when devising their roadmap to a healthier life.

Over the years I began to notice how each guy I played sports with was unique, whether it was how they trained, how they were physically built, or the way they functioned. This became most apparent to me when I got to college. You would see guys who had been training their entire lives or guys who'd never trained a day doing the same routine. The entire team would be squatting, only half did it correctly; the other half never got the help they needed. *Whether it was because they didn't know how to squat properly or couldn't because of muscular imbalances, nothing was done to improve their faults!* That's when I first knew I could change a lot of lives by creating programs specific to an individual's needs.

Some people can find success with a one size fits all approach—but for others it can be their biggest pitfall, particularly with athletes. Either way, the individual will almost never reach their full potential.

After college, I went into teaching, but I found that limited my reach. My ultimate desire was to impact as many lives possible through training – to help them attain goals they'd only dreamed about. I decided to take what I had learned in regards to how the human body functioned and how to identify and fix restrictions, and began working with my brother at the start of his college baseball career. He was later drafted by the Boston Red Sox. Early in his career, they changed his arm-slot in his pitching delivery, significantly decreasing his velocity. Then they did it about five more times. Through training specifically tailored to his delivery, we were able to get him back to his base velocity.

Seeing the difference it made in my brother's performance on the field further reinforced my original belief—people will succeed if they have programs designed specifically to them. Now, whenever I'm training a client, whether it is an athlete or your average Joe or Jane, I am driven by this vision:

I want to impact as many lives as I can. I want to be able to look back and say, "I made a difference for this person or that one," but still be able to see the millions who I haven't met that have tried a litany of ways to reach their goals, but still can't gain ground.

The ability to translate my expertise to help an athlete head to their dream college or assist their parents in bringing back the energy of their youth, has been the driving force for my continued accomplishments.

FINDING YOUR BALANCE

Whether you are an athlete or a soccer mom, you have developed muscular imbalances.

Throughout the course of our lives, everything we do on a daily basis leads to some areas of our body developing more than others. Our human nature is to focus on what we're good at, but often that's at the expense of other areas. You're only as strong as your weakest link. If your contractor wants to build you a top-end home with an insufficient foundation, will you feel comfortable? Of course not. So why would you do that when it comes to your strength programs? All you're doing is developing strength on top of dysfunction. *Everyone has the capacity to become better physically in some way—you just need the proper guidance.*

There are multiple imbalances we encounter when we assess clients:

- Quad dominance
- Shoulder stability
- Core strength and stability
- Posterior chain development
- Dorsi-flexion issues
- Internal-External shoulder-hip rotation deficits
- Thoracic mobility issues
- Hip flexor length/mobility
- . . . among others

As I mentioned earlier, we are all different. Not everyone suffers from all of these issues, but by targeting their specific needs we help to make them well-rounded, which will lead to success.

For example, an imbalance we frequently encounter is an underdeveloped posterior chain, resulting in quad dominance. An underdeveloped posterior chain can lead to knee injuries, poor squat patterns, and underperforming in athletics. For those concerned with appearances, it also leads to a flat backside—*something no woman wants!* Thankfully, there are ways to fix that issue, and once we do you'll be able to:

- Activate your glutes and hamstrings for a higher level of sports performance.

- Utilize your entire lower half, activating muscles you didn't previously use, which allows you to burn more calories for weight loss (the more muscles you use, the more calories you burn).

Too often, people fall into the trap of doing a certain exercise or "cookie-cutter" program to become better physically. *The solutions are seldom that simple...because we are all different!* 4 steps can help you make real changes that solve your equally real problems. When I work with clients, together we:

1. Establish short and long term goals.

2. Define the issue(s).

3. Fix the issue(s) through proper training.

4. Watch the goals come to fruition!

Even if we think about weight loss or sports performance on the most basic level, by creating a plan with the four steps above in mind, we make the goals easier to attain and work towards optimal results because less pain and increased muscle activation equate to healthier weight loss and stronger athletic performances.

When we fix the underlying issues first, we prevent building strength on top of dysfunction and start moving toward our ultimate strength and/or weight loss goals.

SUCCESS SESSIONS: CREATING A CUSTOMIZED TRAINING PROGRAM

By being vested in a client's success, you forge an encouraging and genuine relationship built on mutual excitement for the achievement of an individual's goals.

Success is more than just a definition. When I began Infinite Fitness, the drive for success stemmed from the desire to fully understand and recognize the goals of every client who came through the door and find the best process to get their desired results. With the **Success Session**, we become masterful communicators, as well as showcase our high level of expertise in strength and fitness. We work closely with clients to gain insight into their adversities, fears, and goals so we can create a program for success!

The Five Key Components of a Success Session are:

1. Develop your relationship with your client.

It's more than likely that you haven't met the prospective client before this assessment, so how can you tell them what they need when you don't know a thing about them? When you go to a see a doctor about an illness, would it make sense for him or her to prescribe medicine for you without knowing anything about your symptoms or your lifestyle?

Another statement I live by is, "People don't care what you know, until they first know that you care." You should be willing to take the extra step to learn about your clients, their goals, their weaknesses, etc., in order to establish the best programs for them. If you don't do this first, a client should seek a better facility to train at—one with a team that is willing to build a relationship geared toward success.

2. Set goals.

A strong goal starts with "I will," and is more than just a blanket "I hope to..." statement. It is measurable and has details that help make it more tangible. With the goals that we set, people understand what it is they will achieve.

Recognition that the goal **WILL BE** accomplished is part of specific goal setting. You must establish specific times for when you will achieve each goal. By setting hard deadlines for the short term goals, you will be able to track your progress toward the long term goals.

3. Go through an in-depth assessment.

It's imperative to look at stability and mobility issues, hip and shoulder range of motion, movement patterns, and other aspects of the human body. This is all part of the assessment. The program must reflect these findings and factor them into everything that is done to achieve success.

There are times when elbow pain can be caused by hip issues or back pain can be caused by weak glutes. There is no way to know for certain without an in-depth assessment. If you want to improve, do so based on facts, not speculation.

In some cases, we've even found that training with us isn't an option in the short term. We've found ways to break through this challenge by working closely with physical therapists and orthopedic surgeons to deal with clients who aren't physically ready to start strength and conditioning yet. It's not about simply selling a program. Our philosophy is: "Do enough good things for enough people and good things will happen for you."

4. Create a roadmap for success.

The value of the roadmap is that it is based on specific goals, needs, and limitations; it involves more than weigh-ins and measurements. Based on what's discovered from the previous three steps, we then create the roadmap to achieve the goals.

Once the roadmap is set, it's up to the individual to work with their coach(es) so they may progress toward each short-term goal. You can take one step forward, or backward, each day. If you take one step forward everyday for a year, you will finish 365 steps closer than you were when you started.

Again, to reiterate, this step should be individualized to have success—much like everything else discussed to this point.

5. Be the Coach that never quits!

Being a Coach to clients in pursuit of physical goals is more than just an initial "rah-rah session." It's consistently being there and making sure that you are setting people up to succeed, along with building rapport and trust. We want them to come to the gym inspired, leave excited, and wake up with that same mind-frame again everyday. They must know that they can achieve success—even if it's at the most basic level of their roadmap. It makes all the difference! And there is one thing you cannot fake for long—a genuine spirit for caring. You have to care and that's one thing that I'm so excited about with the Infinite Fitness team; there is no denying that we work from the heart and have the passion to change the lives of everyone that walks through our door.

JOHN'S STORY

My clients are the way I define my success. I love the opportunity to take on the "impossible" or "unknown" to help people realize the root of their physical concerns. It's a new challenge every time, and I never give up on those who come to me in need.

Recently I had a client, John, who came to me with a recurring hamstring injury. He'd seen an orthopedic, who diagnosed it as a partial tear that would only be repaired through rest and stretching. Fast-forward six months later, after following doctor's orders, he was still in the same boat. This was tough because John was a runner. It was his favorite thing to do.

During his assessment, we discovered his hamstring was fine and it was actually one of his hip-extensor muscles that was compromised. Based upon the findings, we developed a roadmap to get John back on his feet. About three weeks later, he met with the orthopedic and explained our diagnosis to him. The doctor decided to run an MRI and the results confirmed what we had found. We continued to train him, and in less than three months he was out running again and hasn't stopped since.

A couple years later, John referred his wife to Infinite. She was very active, and an avid swimmer. She suffered a major shoulder injury that left her with multiple rounds of failed physical therapy. She'd run out of options and came to us as her last resort. She expressed that she understood swimming was probably out of the question, but wanted to improve her quality of life. Approximately ten weeks later she was back in the water!

This couple's experience is what we strive for with every client we deal with, and is why the Infinite name continues to stay relevant. We pride ourselves on not only using our knowledge of the human body, but also on our ability to connect with people to help them get the most from their training experience.

REACHING OUT TO THE WORLD

Every day I work toward one of my biggest goals—changing the lives of people across the globe via proper training and nutrition.

Through my devotion and unwavering passion to bring about action-driven, customized approaches to performance for world-class and amateur athletes, as well as for anyone who has a desire to become better physically, I have witnessed how much of an influence proper programming has on achieving goals. My team and I eagerly embrace the fact that most people have a desire for a more positive life experience and that is gained through a higher level of fitness.

My years of intense focus on the career that I have a deep passion for have opened doors for me to reach people on a global level now. People have travelled to meet me from different countries and I am now able to reach out to them through public speaking—creating a virtual environment where I can train those who are empowered by fitness as a career choice. The opportunities are not stopping, and I don't plan on stopping, either. The more people that I can reach out to and help to understand their body's function and its role in their day-to-day happiness, the better I feel.

Better performance and fitness is and will always be a lifestyle, and we all deserve to reach our true potential.

About Mike

 Mike Fernandes has been changing lives for the last twelve years. Mike was born and raised in Massachusetts. He was a duel sport athlete in high school, excelling in both basketball and baseball. After high school he went on to play baseball at the collegiate level; it was then that he began to realize he wanted to have a positive impact on the lives of others.

Mike originally gravitated to teaching, where he impacted the lives middle school students on a daily basis. At the same time, Mike also worked with high-level athletes, striving towards his lifetime goal of changing the lives of others, but now through fitness and performance.

As more and more people sought Mike out for his training expertise, he decided the only way to continue helping as many people possible, was to open his own training facility. He is the current president and CEO of Infinite Fitness Sports Performance.

Mike's entire teaching and training career has been built around the philosophy that *"people don't care what you know until they first know that you care."* His goal is to build a relationship with every athlete and client that walks through his door. "Once they trust in you and they know you are 100% committed to their success, you can get them to reach levels that they never thought were possible and exceed all expectations." He not only works with all types of athletes, but anyone who is looking to improve their fitness.

As Infinite Fitness Sports Performance has continued to grow, so too has Mike's vision of the impact he can have. Mike retired from teaching after the 2014-2015 school year in order to continue his work on impacting as many lives possible, but on a more global scale, via speaking, training, and nutrition.

Mike has been featured on multiple media platforms both nationally and internationally, including Men's and Women's Fitness, NBC, CBS, and ABC. He has also been recognized as one of America's Premier Experts in his field as well as a World Fitness Elite Game Changer. He is the official strength coach of the New Bedford Bay Sox, a premier collegiate baseball team in the

New England Collegiate Baseball League.

Mike is also the Co-Founder of Elite Training Solutions LLC, an online company focused on changing the lives of people across the globe via nutrition and training.

To book Mike for a speaking engagement or to find out more about him and his mission please visit:
- ifsportsperformance.com
- elite-training-solutions.com
- or facebook.com/infinitefitnessfallriver

CHAPTER 7

STRENGTH STARTS WITHIN YOU

BY JOE BELLISTRI

WHO AM I?

Let me start off by telling you what I am NOT. I am not a medical professional with a psychology degree and a bunch of fancy letters after my name. I am not going to throw out medical jargon in the world of psychosis where you will get lost in my ability to use five-syllable words. Instead, I am going to share my real world experiences, laying out how early life struggles led me down a road of despair without any direction. Leading to troubling times in my life. Then, how these struggles transformed me into the person I am today. And how I used these personal experiences to change my clients' way of thinking and address their own struggles. Which eventually brought them to leading a healthy life and giving them the direction they need to stay on course.

Everyone has their own story of adversity in their lives. We all deal with it differently. These situations can explain why we are who we are. An example is, "Oh poor Chris, he had challenges as a child and is obese because he compensates by overeating." Or they can help define who we want to be and how we want to be recognized. Example, "Chris overcame tremendous obstacles as a child, and now is happy and successful as an adult."

My personal story is not about being overweight as a child and my struggles to lose weight. However, I promise you, the challenges I endured in my life helped me relate to my clients trying to make positive changes and lead a healthier life.

MY STORY

Growing up, I knew that my home life was different than the other kids on my street. My mother suffered from a disease called Friedreich's Ataxia, which is like a distant cousin to Muscular Dystrophy. From an early age, my mother did not have the ability to walk. But, early in my life, she was fairly self-sufficient. She did not let this limitation define her. Our house was filled with cool gadgets that allowed her to get from one floor to another and in and out with no assistance. She had a motorized wheelchair which, back then, was not as available as today. We had a van that was rigged to allow her to drive using hand controls for the gas and brake. It had an electric lift that enabled her to get in and out of the van on her own. As a kid, it was like having a car from the future! We went everywhere.

My mom did not want me to feel like her condition was going to limit her ability to live a "normal life." This woman was my first introduction to inner strength! As we would go places, she was always riding her motorized wheelchair which always drew long looks from passers-by. I remember one time when we were on an elevator at the mall, a woman just kept staring at my mom and her wheelchair. My mother looked up at the woman and said, "Take a picture, it lasts longer." Nice!

Although this helps me paint a nice picture of her confidence, unfortunately this was not always the case. This disease attacks a person's nervous system so her ability to move became more and more limited overtime. And as her body was losing the ability to move, you could see it wearing on her mind. She was plagued with sadness and frustration. Eventually it came to a point where we could not care for her at home. By the time I was 13, she was moved into a nursing home so she could be cared for correctly. She died ten years later, unfortunately suffering along the way.

During the 10 years between my mother's leaving home and her passing, I lived at home with my dad. He was an old school New York City Police Officer that worked the midnight shift. It's probably safe to say, we did not spend a great amount of time discussing our feelings. In fact, not by design, he taught me how to keep things bottled up deep inside. This became my strategy for EVERYTHING! I did not know how to express my feelings, especially the troubling ones. So I kept them inside. I did this for a long time.

Watching my mother slowly die was difficult as a kid and as I grew into a young adult. I didn't know how I was supposed to feel as a kid. Then, as I became a teenager and young adult, I was great at pushing those feelings deep down so I did not have to deal with them. Good plan, right? Wrong!

Holding everything in was not good. I always kept people at an arm's length and never let them in. And if they got too close, I had a knack for pushing people away from me. There were numerous times I would push my longtime girlfriend (now wife "Angela") away, because I was afraid she would eventually leave. I had a very difficult time expressing my emotions and it was frustrating. This led to some significant violent outbursts by me. Throughout college and even those few years after college, all I wanted to do was let out my frustration through physical altercations. Yes, that means getting into fights. As my friends and I would go out to bars on the weekends, my goal was picking a fight. It was getting bad.

I kept running up against adversity. On September 11, 2001, my best friend was one of the 343 New York City firefighters that died at the World Trade Center. A year later my father was diagnosed with pancreatic cancer and was given six months to live (on a positive note, he lived over two years and danced at my wedding reception).

As a teenager and a young adult, these three events had a profound effect on me and my path in life. In truth, it made me afraid to let people in and trust them. In my experiences, everyone that was closest to me left. I also had no direction in life. I struggled with focus in high school and college. I dropped out of college in my sophomore year to try and "find myself." It didn't work. Angela encouraged me to get my Bachelor's Degree. She got me back at school and I again tried to "take a semester off." She did not let me this time. I graduated and made my family proud. But I still had no direction.

I did not have a plan after college. In fact, I did not have a plan for anything. I did not think I would live to see 30 years old. I figured my destructive personality would only take me so far and that would be it. Then everyone would remember me after I was gone and say, "Joe went through a lot when he was young, it was just too much for him."

I was going down the road in which my personal situations explained who I was. I was a troubled kid who not many people would be surprised if he got into trouble in one way or another. I knew what my family and friends were saying about me. Everyone thought I was troubled and could not change. Everyone tiptoed around me. They thought I was crazy! So I decided, I would not let this define me!

How I was perceived bothered me. A lot! I needed to change. *This is the first step to making a change. Recognize that a change is necessary and have the desire to do it.*

With the people that I have the pleasure to work with, this is the first thing we try and uncover. Their "plan" to lead a healthy life was not working. Their desire to change brought them to me. They first recognized they need to change, now we have to uncover the desire to do it. You want to know what it takes. . . **Motivation!**

For me, my motivation started with trying to prove all those people wrong that doubted me. I had a long list throughout my life. It would have to start with my ability to overcome the issues as a kid. I had to be able to talk about things that upset me and express how I felt. Later in life it went on to was I good enough for my wife, was I capable of owning a business, will it be successful, etc. Angela helped me to do that. Not only did it provide clarity in thinking it also calmed down "the bear" inside me. I still use other people's doubts in me to drive me forward. Eventually, I realized that proving people wrong was a negative way to approach motivation. It should be positive. So

I started to look deeper at why I wanted to do things. Being a positive influence on someone was a driving force. Being the best I can be for my family has been a driver for many years. The point is you have to dig deeper to find your motivation for whatever you are trying to do. If your goal is to lose 20 lbs, because you like the way to look in a size 6 might not be enough. For some, that is enough. You have to ask yourself an honest question, "Will it keep you consistent?" Taking clear forward steps to lead a long and healthy life to enjoy your grandkids in retirement. . . now THAT is motivation!

You need to rely on the motivation to keep you **Consistent**. Because we know that life is always going to try to knock us off track. This is where inner belief comes in. In my example, that inner belief helped me to keep my level of communication open with those people closest to me. This kept me calm. For my clients, I try and get them to use their experiences outside of their health to show how strong and committed they really are. Many of them are corporate executives, attorneys, medical professionals, business owners, and amazing parents. They have worked hard in many other facets of their lives to reach their level of success. Imagine an attorney that does not prepare for a court proceeding? An executive that chooses not to go to important meetings? A parent that does not care for their child? Clearly these individuals would not be successful. Now take that mindset and apply it to your health. Figure out the traits that make you successful in your career, school, or home life and find a way to apply them to your health goals (persistent, quick learner, early riser, etc.).

I had a hard time dealing with the last days of both my parents dying. Lying motionless in a hospital bed and watching them slip away. I am not proud to share this, but I gave up on them and was not the best son at the end. This is my greatest regret in life. As a result, I have developed the mantra: **"Never Give Up!"** I use it to motivate myself in my career and with my family. I say this to my kids all the time, "Bellistris never give up!" They buy in and remind each other in times of doubt. I talk to my weight-loss clients about this all the time too. No doubt about it, there will be hurdles along the way. There will be a few weeks where you do not see change. Weight loss is not a linear process, some frustration will set in. The "never give up" mindset will keep you on track until your mission is accomplished. Give it your best effort and you will be proud.

FINAL THOUGHTS

The path to a healthy life requires consistency. You need to lean heavily on your motivation, find it and let it drive you. Whatever you do, never, EVER, give up!

Five Steps to Success
1. Recognize there is an issue
2. Commit to change
3. Identify your motivation
4. Be Consistent
5. Never Give Up

About Joe

 Joe Bellistri is a fitness professional with over 12 years of experience helping his clients achieve their fitness and wellness goals. He takes a comprehensive approach with his clients to drive their results. Its not just about the workout for Joe. Coaching, nutrition and overall motivation are incorporated into his service delivery model.

While he has held a variety of positions at large Corporate gyms over the years, Joe felt that in order to truly take his philosophy to the next level and drive his passion for fitness, he would need to open up his own facility, Solution Fitness. As the owner of **Solution Fitness**, Joe enjoys working with busy professionals offering strategies to lead a healthy life by eating right and exercise. He and his staff also work with student athletes to keep them injury-free and excelling at sports they grew up playing.

Joe believes in simplicity. In his program, he emphasizes that consistency is key. Furthermore, he also works with his clients to help find what truly motivates them to stay focused. This has helped him create a training philosophy that offers safety for his clients and guarantees strategies for continued success.

During his career, he has cultivated relationships with medical professionals that value his expertise in weight loss and corrective exercise. This has made Solution Fitness a viable option for injury prevention and rehabilitation.

Joe Bellistri earned a Bachelor's Degree from St. John's University. His professional certifications include Certified Strength and Conditioning Specialist, Performance Enhancement Specialist, Titleist Performance Institute Certified Golf Fitness Instructor, USA Weightlifting Club Coach, and Certified Function Movement Screen.

Contact information:
www.MySolutionFitness.com

CHAPTER 8

RELEASING THE BRAKES – WHY 'JUST DO IT' THINKING WON'T GET YOU WHAT YOU WANT

BY DAX MOY

How many times have you started a new diet or exercise plan with the best of intentions and resolutions and promising yourself that, 'this time I WILL do this!' only to find that after only a few days (or even hours!) that all of your progress comes to a screeching halt…that your willpower crumbles to dust and that the very things that you promised yourself you wouldn't do are now being done…in supersize?

If you're anything like most people, the answer will be 'HUNDREDS of times' – right?

It's kind of strange when you think about it. On the one hand, we all tell ourselves that losing fat and getting into amazing shape is superimportant to our health and happiness; yet whenever we're asked to prove just how important it really is by being committed and diligent in our efforts, we find it almost impossible to go the distance on our promises.

Why is that?

That's a question I used to ask myself all the time when I first set out on my personal training and coaching career. I'd meet people who would often literally burst into tears in my consulting room – because they were so overcome with pain and emotion as they told me "This MUST change!" and "I'm willing to do ANYTHING it takes to get things right this time" and "I simply cannot take living like this any longer!"

It was seriously moving stuff, and I, of course, believed every word of it. Why wouldn't I? After all, THEY believed every word of it too.

They really and truly believed that 'this time, this ONE time, I'm going to damned-well do this,' yet mere days later (or as much as a week or so for the *really* motivated ones) the first cracks would appear in their resolution and willpower.

One missed workout would become two, two would become three and before they knew what was happening, they were back to not working out at all. Same with nutrition and diet as the 'just one won't hurt' mentality asserted itself and was once again proven wrong. One cookie became two, two became a packet and a packet became licence to say, *"Well, now that I've messed up again, what's the point of carrying on?"*

As a trainer and a coach, this left me floating between genuine confusion about what was going on and frustration about never being able to find 'serious clients,' to (I'm ashamed to admit), anger and resentment toward those who I felt were wasting my time and efforts and deliberately trying to make me look bad. (Irrational, I know, yet it often felt that way at the time.)

Then I realised that the fitness and motivational industries had done a real number on both personal trainers and the clients they serve.

Trainers were told that if a client really and truly wants results, they'd do what's asked of them, no questions asked...and that, of course, if they didn't, that they were wasting both their own time and their trainers' because they simply weren't serious enough about getting results. At the same time, those who were trying to lose weight and get into shape were being made to feel that they were lazy, unmotivated and so stupid that they couldn't figure out that an apple was a better choice of snack than a chocolate bar.

In short, getting into great shape was becoming a lose-lose proposition for all concerned. And one that was adversarial in nature too. Trainers were fighting a battle against 'lazy' clients and clients were in combat with diets and exercise programs they hated, and that simply didn't work for them.

The trouble was, despite all this battling, no one was winning... and they couldn't.

So, against the backdrop of all this battling, I realised something that no one else seemed to be talking about. **The way we were approaching fitness and health simply was not working anymore...and perhaps it never did!**

The idea of eating less and moving more sounds so simple and obvious, yet so few people seemed able to pull this off in any way whatsoever, and those that did only managed it for a short period of time at best.

It struck me then that all of the motivational 'just do it... winners never quit and quitters never win... if you can conceive it and believe it you can achieve it' quotes in the world simply weren't working either. 'Just do it' sounded great, but what if 'doing it' is what you're struggling with most of all?

'Winners never quit' sounds cool too, but what if you've never seen yourself as a winner and have never experienced winning in the first place?

'Conceive, believe, achieve' sounds amazing, but what if you really DON'T believe?

No-one was asking these questions, let alone trying to answer them. Instead it seemed that we were simply insisting that accomplishment and achievement was as simple as living the quotes...even though so few seemed to be able to do so.

So I made it my business to find the answers. And I realised something pretty quickly...

Most of the failures, struggle, stresses and problems we face in pursuing our goals lie not in the goals themselves (pretty much any goal is achievable when you break it down into logical steps), but rather in the fact that we fail to do the one thing that is guaranteed to help us succeed in our quest to reach them. Trouble is, failing to do that one thing guarantees that we never will!

The one thing?

WE FORGET TO RELEASE THE BRAKES.

Picture this...

> You get into your car, start the engine, put your foot on the gas and... nothing. No movement at all, just the noise of the engine turning over.

> Confused, you check that the car is in gear, hit the gas a little harder and hear the engine give a satisfying roar as the revs increase – yet once more, nothing. You're going nowhere.

> Frustrated now, you floor the gas, the engine screams, the whole car vibrates and starts to roll forward just a little as bit by bit, the power of the engine overcomes the inertia of a ton of glass, metal and upholstery, yet because you're concerned about the noise coming from the engine, the smell of burning rubber coming from the wheels and the intense vibration coming from everywhere you decide to stop....to quit...you'll take your journey another day, you decide.

> Just as you're about to switch off the engine and call your mechanic, you look down and experience a Homer Simpson 'Doh!' moment as you realise that you still had your parking brake in place. No wonder you weren't going anywhere!

> You release the brake, lightly tap the gas and roll easily and quietly out of the driveway and set out for your destination... at last!

Why the story about cars and brakes?

Because it describes EXACTLY why most of your fitness and fatloss attempts fall flat on their face. In your effort to 'just do it', you're setting out on your journey without doing the most important thing you could possibly do to assure your success.

You're setting out without releasing the brakes!

— Starting a diet while you still have processed, high sugar, high carb food in your cupboards and refrigerator?

Brake!

If you own it you WILL eat it.

— Starting an exercise program without setting aside specific times to exercise?

Brake!

If you can't say EXACTLY when your training will take place, then you're unlikely to train at all. 'Today' or 'later' isn't the same as '6:15 am every day' for example.

— Setting out without a clear purpose and a deep and meaningful reason for pursuing them?

Brake!

A big enough 'why' will keep you on the straight and narrow when times get tough, yet a small one (or none at all) will guarantee you'll quit every time.

These are just 3 examples, yet they clearly show how most attempts at getting into great shape are lost before they even get started, as driving with the brakes on is simply too hard, too tiring, too boring and lack any real power to make anyone want to commit to doing the work required to get the results.

On the other hand, releasing the brakes makes it all very easy for the simple reason that all of your efforts can be used to move you forward – rather than having to fight against the pull of those things that are holding you back.

You 'get' this, right? But how do you actually implement releasing the brakes so that you can benefit from all the forward momentum you're going to gain?

Easy!

Simply identify the biggest 3-5 brakes in each of the following areas:

- **Time** – what time brakes are keeping you from doing what you need to do in order to get the results you want to get? Where is time being used poorly? Where is time being wasted? What could you do to get more time?

- **Inspiration** – what kind of things are present in your life that are sapping your motivation and inspiration? What 'motivation thieves' are currently making life harder for you than it could and should be?

- **Clarity** – what are you not clear about, need to learn more about or want more information about? Lack of clarity is a BIG brake!

- **Relationships** – what relationship brakes are present that are making it hard to focus on your goal? WHO is getting in the way of your progress?

- **Nutrition** – what nutrition brakes are in your way that are keeping you from achieving your goal? Too many carbs? Processed foods? Snacking?

- **Exercise** – What elements of your exercise program are acting like brakes? Exercises you don't like? Gym you hate? Program that takes too long?

Once you've identified at least 3 brakes in each area, identify WHY they are brakes and how they actually affect your ability to progress toward your goals.

For instance, a relationship brake may be that you feel guilty about leaving your family for an hour in the evening while you go to the gym, because they already see so little of you due to work commitments. An exercise brake may be that you can't stand cardio training because everyone tells you that you have to do it to get results, and because of this you don't end up training at all.

Identify why each brake IS a brake and how the brake actually stops you: "I feel guilty leaving the house again after getting home from work, so I stay home with the family instead, but end up doing nothing but sitting on the sofa, watching TV, eating…and getting fatter."

It's important that you tell the truth, the whole truth and nothing but the truth while answering these questions. After all, the truth will set you free…as you'll soon see!

Finally, come up with 3-5 solutions that allow you to release each brake in each area where you're stuck.

Feel guilty about coming home late then going back out again?

Could you get up earlier and hit the gym on the way to work? Could you buy some fitness equipment and train at home? Could you make it fun and engage your kids in your plans to get into great shape?

In all 3 examples above, there's a solution for releasing the brakes. Pick one, or better still, create your own.

Do this for all of the primary brakes before you even think of putting your foot 'on the gas' and getting going in pursuit of your goals.

I know what you're thinking. Sounds like a lot of work, right? Maybe, but so is failing. So is starting but never finishing. So is never ever seeing the results you so desperately want to see in return for all your efforts.

Yet the 30 minutes this exercise will take to complete can change your life. Just 30 minutes and the brakes will release and with less effort than ever before you'll be moving along in the direction of your goals.

Just 30 minutes.

Ask the questions. Answer the answers.

Release the brakes and no matter how big your goal, your success is guaranteed…you'll see!

About Dax

Dax Moy is the guy you call when your dreams are too small. A best-selling author with several titles related to self-development, personal growth, goal-achievement and holistic health as well as being a recognised member of The World Fitness Elite, Dax is a worldrenowned expert in human performance – who is regularly sought out for his opinions on developing performance strategies that really work.

Dax has been seen on BBC News, ITV's "This Morning" Show, Ch4's "You Are What You Eat", *CBS News* and in *The New York Times, The Washington Post, The Financial Times, The Evening Standard* and magazines such as *Men's Health, Men's Fitness, Health and Fitness, Glamour, Vogue* and *Cosmopolitan* among many others.

Dax is known as a coach who's dedicated to bringing out the greatness in others through his laser-focused ability to ask the questions that count, and finding the answers that inspire rapid and dramatic change in his clientele. His clientele includes Royalty, A-list celebrities, Actors, Musicians, Politicians and CEO's.

To learn more about Dax Moy –"The Guy You Call When Your Dreams are Too Small," and to get a copy of his special report, *The Biggest Lie - The TRUTH About Why Your Life Isn't Working Out,* visit: www.IAmDaxMoy.com

CHAPTER 9

THE MISSION OF MINDSET: 5 STEPS TO TOTAL LIFE AND BODY TRANSFORMATION

BY CHAD MOELLER

My story of fitness started back when I was in first grade. It was just after a game of dodge ball, the class was divided into equal teams and I remember clearly that I was the only one left on my team and the other team had hardly anyone gone with about 15 kids against me. I was an underdog and came back completely... Catching balls, dodging throws, eliminating others, and going on to win for my team. The Physical Education teacher pulled me aside after class and told me. "You have something special kid, you are going to grow up to be an amazing athlete." That was a strong seed planted in my first-grader mind. That one statement as a child formed a belief I believed to be true and made a huge impact on my personal identity, and I did grow up to prove him right. I believed that statement he spoke to me, and ended up in High School as Captain of three sports, went on to play college football at the Division I and II level, and graduated with a degree in Health and Human Performance.

The reason I bring that story up is personal identity (the way we view ourselves), directly impacts our behavior. We behave the way we see ourselves. If you see yourself as overweight and unhealthy you are going to behave like that person. Same holds true with positive identity. A great example of someone trying to accomplish something with a personal identity that is not congruent to their goals is a New Years Resolutioner! This seems to be the time of the year where people get highly motivated to make a positive change. They set their sites on a goal, they make great strides in working towards it, they start seeing the results, they start making an impact on their health, but then they backslide; they down a bottle of wine, they have episodes of binge eating at night, they skip workouts and make excuses.

The crazy thing about it is that they know the actions to take and the path to follow, yet they still sabotage their own success! The reason for this is their own identity drives behavior. They are behaving like they see themselves and it pulls them back to that image. I like to use the analogy of swimming in a river. When you attack a goal without making your identity congruent with it first, you are swimming against the current in the river, and eventually that current will wear you out enough where it carries you back. However, when your identity is in line with your goals you are swimming with the current and now you are achieving things faster, and making changes that last, letting that current carry you on to the positive way you see your self.

My personal development of mindset has been a work in progress. I have been highly influenced by a lot of the greats. . . Wayne Dyer, Brian Tracy, BJ Ganem, Napoleon Hill, Tony Robbins, and Maxwell Maltz, to name a few. And collectively, I have stood on the "Shoulder of these Giants" to create a process for my clients to unlock their potential. No one person has all the answers, and what I am about to share with you came from a community of high performers, therefore you might recognize some of the ideas and concepts. I have put together what I have learned from the greats and organized them into a format to help my clients succeed.

I feel the most important component is having a strong identity. The fact I am even an author communicating to you came as a result of the 5-step process I am going to share with you. I want to share a few quick success stories of clients of mine that used this mindset process. Travis came in with a goal of making it to the rodeo finals, he knew the odds were stacked against him at the age of 37, but we worked that mindset and he indeed qualified for the finals later that year, beating out people in their 20's to get there. His identity matched his actions and it showed in how he attacked each training session.

Kim, who battled a bad body image since the third grade (now in her late 20's), changed that identity when we unlocked her mindset. She went from a size 16 to a size 6. The last success story means a lot because Mike told me I came along at his darkest hour. The way he saw himself wasn't positive, he had diabetes, and when it came to health and fitness, he felt defeated. I came to speak to the employees at the company he worked at, and after that he reached out to me for help. The first thing we did was change that mindset, the rest followed, he is insulin free. Got one of the best health reports from his doctor since being diagnosed, started playing golf again, lost over 50 pounds, and best of all, his identity is healthy, and every area of his life has improved as a result of that!

I believe whole-heartedly that if you want to reach your full potential in fitness you have to pay attention to mindset. Skipping this chapter and going on to exciting workouts, eating strategies, etc. is probably more fun, but I promise you that if you lay this groundwork you will achieve more!

Why is mindset important for fitness (or anything in life). To answer that, I want to change your perspective. Most people walk around and operate like we are a body with a mind attached, but I want you to think differently. We are actually a mind with a body attached. If you adopt that change in perspective, you will not just become a powerhouse in the gym but also a powerhouse in the mind. Now it doesn't matter how much you read, how many facts you fill your head with, or how much theory you are exposed to. It is not going to hit home until you experience the power in your own life.

If you continue to see yourself as an unfit, unhealthy person you will be continuously "swimming against that current," with thoughts pulling you back to self-sabotaging behaviors. You must change that identity immediately because who you think you are is going to determine the decisions you make and the actions you take in any given situation. To do this effectively, take this **FIVE STEP** approach:

STEP 1: BURN YOUR LIMITING BELIEFS
(Do this step once or as often as needed.)

The first step is making yourself aware of the negative energy and beliefs you are carrying around. We don't realize this, but these negative beliefs, fears and limitations all impact our behavior, and can even bring more undesirable results. I discovered an awesome technique for releasing this energy after attending a conference. Writing these out is extremely cathartic. To get started, you will need three sheets of paper:

1. Write down *Any Toxic Thoughts* that discourage, cause anger, or throw you off track – regarding your health and fitness.

2. Write down *Any Limiting Beliefs* that are holding you back, getting in the way, and sabotaging your success.

3. Write down *Past Failed Attempts* at your health and fitness.

Write down EVERYTHING that comes to mind; be completely open! Find an ashtray, light them on fire and say, "That was then. . . THIS IS NOW!" Feel those things being released from your subconscious mind. They will no longer affect you, EVER again! They are gone. . . gone up in smoke. . . and your new life begins NOW!

STEP 2: UNLOCK YOUR IMAGINATION AND VISUALIZE THE NEW YOU

More and more the things we could experience are lost to us, banished by our failure to imagine them.
~ Rainer Maria Rilke

What you place in your imagination is the most powerful component of this process. Your mind has no limits, the only limits we really have are the self-imposed limits we place in our mind ourselves. Now we have burned and released all the negatives that used to be stuck in our mind, we can now focus on creating the Strong Identity of who we really want to be.

Visualize. Let your mind run free, remove all limits and fears, and truly see the person you want to be. Anything IS possible and that is why I want you to create the mental picture of exactly the person you want to be. Visualize that, hold onto to that image, and believe you are already this person. Do not skip this step, there is a reason the best free throw shooters visualize every shot before they take it, there is a reason why the most successful people use vision boards and "see" their success before they accomplish it. Remember, no limits, no fear. This time go for it, and focus on that image of the new you without holding back!

Now create a "Vision Board." Have fun with this. Find pictures of you when you were in the best shape of your life, find pictures of people who look like the person you want to be – let that inspire you. Part of your new strong identity is not just the success you have with your health and fitness, but also in other areas of life. Often times fitness transformation is the catalyst to life transformation. So put in pictures of things you want to accomplish, of the car you want to drive, the house you want to live in, places you want to travel to, etc.

STEP 3: DESCRIBE YOUR VISUAL IMAGE

To make this more real, sit down and write out every detail of your strong new identity. To help with this, describe how others treat you in this new state, describe how you feel, describe how you look, how you are dressed, how you carry yourself! Then write what actions this new you is taking to achieve this. When you write this stuff out, what you placed in your imagination now begins to reinforce itself because you are bringing meaning and life to the image. This takes it out of your mind and is like breathing existence into your new identity.

When writing this out, there are some key concepts to keep in mind that I learned from the classic book, *Think and Grow Rich*.

1. Stop focusing on what you don't want.

2. Write out what you DO want and be definite and specific about it.

3. Have a strong sense of belief and faith that you are this person as you are writing. (See and feel yourself as this person.)

4. Write as if you are already in possession of your new, strong identity.

STEP 4: ACT AS IF...

Now is the time to behave like the person you have visualized, and described yourself to be. At first this is going to seem unnatural, its kind of like starting a new job, learning to drive stick shift, or learning a new exercise. Well! It is the same thing here. You are "learning" your new Identity. There are four phases in this learning phase.

1. Unconscious Incompetence: (I don't know what I don't know.)

2. Conscience Incompetence: (I know what I don't know.)

3. Conscience Competence: (I apply what I know.) <-- This is where you are at this moment in the process.

4. Unconscious Competence: (I apply what I know without having to think about it.) . . . THIS IS WHERE YOU WILL BE!

Your mind is like a muscle of the body. It is something that needs to be trained, just as an athlete learns a new skill, at first they are sloppy, uncoordinated, and slower, but in time as their muscles get conditioned they master it. The same holds true with your mind and in time you will advance through the four phases.

STEP 5: REINFORCE, REINFORCE, REINFORCE!!!

The more you reinforce, the faster you progress to Unconscious Competence. Embracing and becoming your new, strong identity comes from thoughts and self talk you have about your new identity, visualizing your new identity, reading your written statement as often as possible, and repeating this cycle without missing a day until your new identity becomes a reality at Unconscious Competent level. So I want to give some guidance on this step.

So let's start with your thoughts. Thought is energy, focused thoughts are powerful energy, and focused thoughts soaked with emotion becomes energy that comes to realization. When you repeat your vision with enough repetition and soak it in emotion, you will bring it to life. This is so powerful that we have to be intentional about making sure our self-talk matches our new identity. This is why you see patterns in so many people. Their thoughts tend to go into the same places as always, and therefore they tend to relive or attract a lot of the same circumstances in their life. If they view the world as out to get them, they will subconsciously prove themselves right. So stand guard and use this concept for good, not evil!

Visualize your new identity. Your subconscious is very powerful. It takes things at face value and accepts the visions as real – whether your imagination came up with them or you experience them. It can't tell the difference. . . now is the time to project your ideal body in your mind, let your subconscious soak it up and it will change your actions and rewire your habits. Make sure to make time each morning and each night before bed, to look at and embrace your vision board. This has a compounding effect because it will create new situations, bring you into contact with people that can help make the vision real, and what may seem very coincidental is actually a result of these changes in behavior. If you visualize while you are in a relaxed state, it gets even more embedded into your mind.

In the book *Think and Grow Rich*, author Napoleon Hill suggests that the written statement be read twice daily. Once in the morning and once before retiring to bed. I would say that should be a bare minimum, and only one aspect to this last step. Start each day and actually rewrite the statement. He also suggests to read it out loud, and I believe that gives more impact to the process. One tip I have is to actually rewrite the statement everyday, and then type it out in a document that you can access from your phone. That way, when you think of it, you will have easy access to recite it word for word. While doing this make sure you see, feel and believe, as it has already been accomplished by you.

My hope is that this chapter will help you on the path to total transformation. Remember this:

A total body and life transformation begins and ends with the mind.

About Chad

Chad Moeller has always been committed to the idea that any type of lasting transformation begins with your mindset. He has spent decades learning and developing what is required to take your health, fitness, and life to the next level. Chad's passion for personal development and learning is second only to his desire to help friends, family and clients reach their full potential and gain the confidence they need to make a lasting transformation that changes their life.

Chad, a former collegiate athlete at the Division I & II levels, is still very active in sports and obstacle course racing. He started as a personal trainer in 1997, and has helped thousands of people of all shapes and sizes reach their health and fitness goals. He has a Bachelor's Degree in Health and Human Performance, and multiple national certification designations and awards. Chad strives to enhance the lives of others by communicating the truths and dispelling the myths of health and fitness, for total, lasting transformation in both mind and body.

Chad Moeller has worked with elite athletes, executives, moms, and kids to direct them in achieving the pinnacle of success within their chosen endeavors and personal goals. He has written articles on health and fitness topics including nutrition, strength training, and cardiovascular exercise. Chad is also a brand ambassador for fitness supplements and also runs a highly successful fitness training company.

Whenever Chad is not helping his clients achieve maximum success and confidence, he enjoys biking, boxing, obstacle racing, and spending time with his kids and family.

Learn more at: chadmoellerfitness.com

CHAPTER 10

THE FIRST STEP TO FITNESS SUCCESS

BY PAT RIGSBY

A journey of a thousand miles begins with a single step.
~Lao-tzu

Do you have a fitness goal that you want to pursue? Are you finding it difficult to take that first step toward making this goal a reality? What's holding you back? What has stopped you from taking those first steps to fitness or fat loss success? Here are a few that have affected me at one time or another in the past:

Feeling Overwhelmed. Read the Lao Tzu quote again: 'A journey of a thousand miles begins with a single step.' No matter how large or how small the endeavor, you still have to begin with a single action. You don't have to have it all figured out. Simply take the first step.

Fear of _____. (Fill in the blank.) It could be any number of things. Failure. Humiliation. Loss. Odds are the fear that you're experiencing is far worse than the actual reality, if whatever you're afraid of did happen. 99% of the time, the fear that's holding you back is not that big of a deal. The potential discomfort you'd experience is nothing compared to the elation you'd experience from actually achieving your goal.

Unwilling to Leave the Comfort Zone. This is just a nicer way of saying you're being too lazy to reach your goals. You must accept that achieving anything of significance requires work and dedication. So log out of Facebook, quit texting and hop off the coach and make your dreams happen.

Comparing Ourselves with Others. Your objectives should simply be tied to reaching your own potential. Don't worry about other people and what they've done unless it fuels you to work harder and do more. Otherwise focus on being the best version of you.

Thinking Things Had to Be Perfect. Waiting until the situation is perfect is a direct route to inaction because the situation will never be perfect. No matter how well prepared you are, there will always be something unexpected that pops up, so don't let the need for perfection stand in your way.

Doing More Research. This is just another way of saying 'you're too lazy to do the real work.' As I just mentioned, things don't have to be perfect to get started, so the need for endless research before taking action is completely unfounded.

Not Feeling 'Worthy' Enough. Not believing that you had enough education, knowledge, skill or experience can stop you before you get started, but the truth is that you can get experience without 'doing' and you can't develop your skill without practice. Most every 'expert' I know felt this way at one point or another and still proceeded to take action. So should you.

If you're like me, the seven things that I listed above have at one time or another stood between inaction and action. But they're all just small obstacles designed to separate the haves from the have-nots. The successful from the average. The real bottom line is this: no matter what your goal is, the best time to start is now.

I learned this back when I became a college baseball coach at the ripe old age of 23. At that point I was the youngest collegiate head coach in the country and felt a version of all seven things I listed previously:

• Becoming a head coach was completely overwhelming for

someone who'd just graduated college a few months before. Being responsible for over 30 young men and a collegiate athletic program was far more responsibility than I'd ever had before.

• I was afraid of failure and humiliation. The program had never had a winning season prior to my taking over in spite of being led by two well known and previously successful coaches, so the odds were stacked against me and I was worried about doing so poorly that I'd be fired and ruin any chance of getting another job in coaching.

• It's easy to say, 'I'd like to be a college coach' but actually stepping up and applying and potentially being rejected was something that I struggled with.

• I looked at all the coaches of the programs I'd be coaching against and it was obvious that they were far more experienced, more knowledgeable and had superior resources. I also took notice of the two previous coaches who held the position that I was applying for and recognized that by most any standard they were far superior to me as a coach.

• I knew that the circumstances I was potentially entering were not ideal. A program with poor resources, a limited budget and no track record of success wasn't exactly the ideal launching pad for a successful career.

• Most 23-year-olds that were interested in being a baseball coach were taking positions as Assistant Coaches for High School JV Teams, not going after Collegiate Head Coaching jobs. Why should I be any different?

But ultimately I accepted the premise above:

THE BEST TIME TO START IS NOW!

And I learned as I went. When I started coaching, I didn't know how to run a practice, how to motivate players or how to recruit effectively.

But I accepted the challenge and started the job anyway. The first few months were really tough. After my first season I still hadn't 'found myself' as a coach. We had a winning season (barely), the first in school history in my first year, but it was more of a throwing-stuff-against-the-wall-to-see-what-sticks approach than actually figuring things out.

Thankfully, the experience taught me a lot. The next year the team did better. By the third season we were nationally ranked, and in the fifth season we finished fifth at the World Series.

And none of this would have happened unless I took the first step in spite of my insecurities.

And what I learned through that experience has benefited me time and time again.

No matter what your goal, success is a process and it requires overcoming limiting beliefs and taking action.

Maybe your goal is to lose 30 pounds of unwanted weight. Perhaps it's to fit back into your 'skinny jeans' this fall or to run a 10K race in the Spring. Maybe your goals are loftier. You might want to run a marathon or win a 5K. Maybe you want to compete in a powerlifting meeting or a figure competition. You might even want to follow your passion and move into a career as a fitness professional and even have your byline in a popular magazine.

It really doesn't matter whether you want to lose 10 pounds or 100, walk your first 5K or win your next half-marathon. Actually, I'd encourage you to dream big and set lofty goals for yourself. That's part of what makes life worth living. But you must understand, the key isn't so much what the goal is, but how you act on it.

Once you've set your goal, big or small, you will do much, much better if you spend more time thinking about your 'first steps' than just the big picture dreams and goals that you've laid out.

Just recently while doing a coaching session with a client of mine, I suggested that in addition to the big dreams he had set out for himself, I wondered if he might also benefit from having some realistic goals for the short term. I then proceeded to suggest a few.

While I don't know your particular 'big goals', here are a few example first step goals that will help you generate momentum and start making real progress toward where you want to be:

- If you want to run a 10K but are new to running, consider beginning with a light jog to the end of the street followed by 30 minutes of brisk walking.

- If you want to lose 50 pounds, start with doing 30 minutes of exercise each day.

- If you want to overhaul your diet, start by making one change like committing to eating a supportive breakfast every day.

- If you want to do a triathlon but are just starting out, commit to biking, swimming and running each twice per week.

To someone who has been exercising for quite some time, an advanced runner or a competitive triathlete, these kinds of goals might seem rather small and insignificant – but for a newbie they'd be a good start.

For someone who is just starting but not deconditioned, these smaller goals might seem a little insignificant also. However, I'd argue that to get to your big dreams there are a lot of steps in between. And many of those steps might not be as exciting or as fun to think about as the big endpoint you've identified as your ideal destination. But often it's important to focus on the very next steps that you need to take in order to move towards your goals. This is how you generate momentum. By putting one foot in front of the other. By getting up to workout in the morning when you don't feel like it. By eating a healthy breakfast when doughnuts sound far better.

Success isn't a big leap. It's the combination of hundreds or even thousands of little steps in succession. But most people don't recognize that, so they look for the magic bullet. The quick fix. And while this isn't good news if you're looking for immediate gratification, it's great news if you're willing to start stepping. Because you understand that the magic is in the process and the process begins with that first step.

And don't think that you're stuck taking what you may feel are baby steps for long. Once you've achieved these first small goals, start to increase them. You might want to go from jogging down the street to running around the block. Then for a mile without stopping. Then another. Before you know it, you've put a series of steps together and you're well on your way to achieving your big goal.

But before you can run, you need to walk.

So to quote Dr. Denis Waitley – "There never was a winner who was not first a beginner."

The most important thing you can do to make your goals a reality is that first step.

About Pat

In the past decade, Pat Rigsby has built over a dozen businesses as a CEO and Co-Owner, with five becoming million dollar or multi-million dollar ventures. Two of those businesses, Athletic Revolution and Fitness Revolution, have been multiple-time winners on the Entrepreneur Franchise 500 with each being the #1 franchise for it's respective market. Another business, Fitness Consulting Group, was a multiple time honoree on the Inc. 5000, placing as high as #580 on the list of fastest growing businesses in the U.S. He's also been a Best-Selling Author six times over, presented in front of thousands of entrepreneurs and been featured in *Entrepreneur, Men's Health, USA Today* and on hundreds of other media outlets.

When it comes to sales, Pat's personally sold as many as 116 franchises in a single year and been the strategist and copywriter for over 10 million dollars in online sales from his own businesses and millions more in sales for his clients.

Pat's coaching and consulting clients have been featured in places like *Men's Health, USA Today, Men's Fitness, Shape, Women's Health, Huffington Post* and on ABC, CBS, NBC television affiliates and pretty much any other media outlet you can think of. In addition to that, they've built some of the most successful businesses and brands in every corner of the industry, from local business and supplement companies to online businesses, certification organizations and have even became best selling authors. In fact, many (if not most) of the experts providing business coaching in the fitness industry have been his clients, customers or franchisees.

And the best part of this? He's been able to do all of these things and more while working from home, coaching his kids in baseball and soccer and enjoying a type of entrepreneurial lifestyle he would have never thought possible just a few short years ago.

If you'd like to see how you might be able to work together with Pat, you can reach him at: pat@patrigsby.com.

CHAPTER 11

GET OFF THE SCALE TO GET RESULTS

BY HOLLY RIGSBY

How many times are you doing it? Once a week...once a day...several times a day?

Stepping on the scale – wishing, hoping, praying as you hold your breath and stare down at the number you see above your toes, almost afraid to look. Wondering why, despite your efforts to eat right and exercise, this number will not budge – or worse, only goes up!

Have you ever stopped to realize how this obsession with a number on the scale is actually holding you back from making progress?

Sure we all begin a fitness plan with the ultimate goal to drop some weight, however when it comes to the process women must go through to get results, many get caught up with the number on the scale, and end up losing sight of the most important changes that are taking place – ones that a scale simply cannot measure.

I'd like to share a story from a mom I have worked with since the start of 2011 who broke her addiction to the scale. Her story hits home for I can personally relate to the struggles she experienced as she strived to get results and achieve a fit and healthy body. Her transformation also demonstrates the potential we all have to transform, when we take the power away from the scale and begin to focus on the success that truly does matter – to true and lasting body shaping results.

I'll now turn it over to Niki.

"Never in a million years would I have ever been convinced that breaking free from the scale would allow me to drop 2 sizes and completely reshape my body.

Believe it or not…. before I began my Fit Yummy Mummy transformation, I was broken, lost and unhealthy. My journey had started, like so many other moms, after having my son. I'm embarrassed to say that I weighed a whopping 197 lbs. on the day I gave birth. At that point, I knew that it was going to be a struggle to lose the baby weight.

I ended up working on my body for 8 years! After dozens of failed at- tempts with fad diets, diet pills and even joining a health club…I felt like nothing was going to work for me. I would do great for a few weeks and then right after the scale started to move, I would quit – and the weight came back on.

In my eyes, nothing worked and I always failed.

I was forever searching for "the" program that was going to do it for me…. the program that was going to help me lose those stubborn pounds, because then I would be skinny.

My self-esteem was also at an all time low. I truly believed that the answer to all my life's problems at that time was held in that number that was on the scale. I became obsessed with that number, weighing progress, success and who I was, fully based on that number.

I was a slave to the scale.

I was always thinking about the pounds I wanted to lose, the size I wanted to be and the figure that I longed to have. I thought that if I could just lose that weight and be skinny that I could finally be happy, beautiful, care free, desirable. What I didn't fully understand was the underlying issue. I hated….ME.

Prior to signing up for ClubFYM in November of 2010, I had lost enough weight to reach 134 – I thought this would make me happy, but I was still round and jiggly, and I still couldn't shake a size 8.

I was doing cardio a LOT along with some workout DVDs. I'd even add in power-walks several times per week! In my mind I kept thinking that all this exercise should be making me skinny!!!

I was so frustrated with "all my efforts" and my inability to lose any more weight. I thought that it was SO UNFAIR! What I didn't realize is that I didn't have a clue how to be healthy.

I had originally purchased the Fit Yummy Mummy eBook and interval soundtracks in the spring of 2010. I had gotten Holly's emails for over a year, so I finally decided to join ClubFYM in November of 2010, because something told me that I needed more. There was something missing. To me, at that point, the missing piece was weight loss. Plus I had NO intention of doing a 'challenge,' because at that point, I thought it wasn't for me at all and would be a waste of my time. And I had no time or interest in the forums.

January 2011 – it all changed.

I just knew that this year was going to be different. It was going to be amazing. I didn't know how or why. I just knew. So I decided on a total whim to join the New Year's Transformation Challenge.

Previously, I had found challenges to be silly. I now realize it was all my insecurity of actually being able to accomplish anything I set out to do. But something inside told me that I needed to give it a try this time. What was even greater was my desire to purchase the Transformation Kit, since it had everything I needed to do, laid out step-by-step.

While my goal was to lose weight and eat right, I also thought I should really work on my self-esteem.

What I went through in 12 weeks was a journey of self-discovery and healing.

In working on my external appearance, I discovered that so many of the reasons I was lacking in results, my self-worth was wrapped up in issues I needed to deal with from my past. Without even trying, I found myself reflecting and discussing my journey.

I was constantly asking myself "why?" And when I thought I had found the answer, I would go back and reflect more. This was happening while I was learning the FYM lifestyle of the right way to eat, and the best ways to workout.

By the time my 12 weeks were complete, what I found was new respect for myself!

I broke free from the scale and from the chains that had been holding me back. I was able kick my negative self-image to the curb. When I was done with the challenge, I actually saw myself through new eyes.

I saw a woman that had features she had never had before. Confidence. Pride. Self-worth. Beauty. Love. Respect.

The biggest eye opener was that the scale barely budged. In 12 weeks, I only lost 2 pounds! However, I was able to lose 13 overall inches and dropped from a size 7/8 to a size 3/4.

Here are my 12 week results...
   Weight: 130 - 128 Size: 7/8 - 3/4
   Mommy Tummy: 31 - 27.5
   Hips: 37.5 - 36
   Thighs: 22.5 - 20.5

A size 3/4! I have NEVER been this size in my life! I remember wearing a size 7/8 in 6th grade. What I didn't realize was that looking in the mirror each day, I always saw the same thing – my shape. What I discovered was that although my shape was still the same, my SIZE was not! Talk about an eye opener! Another shock for this scale addict!

This is only the beginning of my new journey. I still have goals to meet, but that's the way I like it. It gives me something to work toward. I'll always have that next leg of my journey. I'm a work in progress and that motivates me! And when life throws me a curveball, I know that it won't derail me. I just work through it, and go back to where I was before.

What matters most is that I officially broke free from the scale and am now ready to take part in the next challenge. I have never felt more amazing, vibrant, healthy, energized and alive! Gone are the negative thoughts and the jello-jiggler wiggle. I am a new me and proud of it! My experience with Fit Yummy Mummy at this point is not so much about what I lost, but rather what I gained!

I gained an incredible amount of respect and knowledge about myself. I learned how strong I am both internally and externally. And most im- portantly, what I found during this transformation was something that I didn't even know I was looking for at the beginning......ME."

- Niki Baklund, Age 31, Mom of 8 year old son; Hutchinson, Minnesota – Fit Yummy Mummy since January 2011 and Proud Member of ClubFYM

Just like Niki, I too used to give the scale way too much power. Looking back I see that not only did this number dictate the mood of my day, it also lead me to engage in unhealthy habits that gave me the false sense that I was able to be in control of keeping this number as low as possible. This exhausting routine only resulted in damaging my metabolism and even worse, my self-esteem. Looking back I now see that I was a slave to the scale and I truly am more than just a number.

Now to help you get past this obsession with the scale, I'd like to ask you a question.

Ready?

"Would you like to weigh less or take up less space?"

Take a moment to really think about this one. You are all here to lose FAT, right? In order to make this happen there are fundamental fat loss factors that must be in place: eating supportively, effective strength training plan, intervals instead of long hours of cardio and of course, an attitude programmed for success.

The most unfortunate part of the fat loss process is that many women give up, quit and believe they are destined to be overweight, for they cannot get the scale to budge. This is a devastating path to take and can be very easily avoided when you simply understand what is happening, and know what to look for.

Why is the Scale an ineffective measure of success?

It CANNOT show you the change in your body composition - the loss of fat and the increase in lean muscle. As you gain some lean muscle and lose some fat, the numbers on the scale do not initially change.... but magically, your clothes are no longer snug - what is happening?

First let me quickly clear up the Muscle vs. Fat Controversy. Pure fat is around 0.9g per cubic centimeter, while muscle is around 1.1g per cubic centimeter. In other words....muscle is leaner and tighter than fat.

And yes, muscle is super-important to your body-shaping goals. Increasing your lean muscle:

1. Burns more fat
2. Boosts your metabolism
3. Allows you to fit comfortably into your skinny jeans
4. Increases your strength
5. Increases bone density
6. Makes you look lean, toned and defined

When fat is decreased on the body and slight muscle gains take place by following a full body-strength training program, it creates a more fit, lean, toned and attractive look.

It's past time to get off the scale. Why would anyone put all this effort into changing how to eat, how to workout and how to live each and every day for nothing in return? No one would. But we all crave and NEED some type of feedback. Crazy cool thing is – you already have it!

Throughout your weight loss efforts, have you at one time or another noticed....

- A melting away of inches
- A barrage of compliments - others are noticing a pleasant

change not only in your appearance but in your overall attitude

- A tremendous amount of energy
- The ability to DO more than you ever could before
- An amazing amount of *self confidence*

Now, another question for you.... Has a scale EVER given you the feedback I have just listed above?

No, and it never will. Stop beating yourself up and step OFF the scale.

Instead focus on what DOES measure and create momentum for successful results.

How?

Take circumference measurements, use your skinny jeans and take "before" pictures. Why? Because you can see them. As your fitness level improves, as your strength increases, as you drop a jean size, does it really matter what the scale says?

If you really think about it, a rational person would be totally willing to gain a few pounds in exchange for losing an inch in their soft and squishy spots. Get this...my body today – after 2 babies – is now 16 pounds heavier than when I was addicted to the scale and doing everything I could to control this number.

Just like so many other things that have changed in my life as I have found my passion and paved the way for Fit Yummy Mummy to reach moms around the world, so did this! My scale has been retired for a while and it has been one of the best things I've done. It is my hope that you too will put it up for a time and focus on the changes that truly matter to your long-term results.

At the end of the day, it's your life that can change the scale, not the other way around.

Change your perspective to something healthier – change your body forever!

About Holly

 Holly Rigsby is The Fit Yummy Mummy and Busy Mom Fat Loss Expert.

Holly is an ACE certified personal trainer, Kettlebell Athletics Certified and author of FitYummyMummy. com the 16 Week Fat Loss System designed Exclusively for Busy Moms, helping moms burn the baby fat with 15-minute workouts that can be performed at home. Holly launched this exciting fat loss plan for Moms in 2007 after going through her own personal post baby transformation.

Holly has since created a number of fat loss tools in an effort to simplify body-shaping results for moms, including the comprehensive Transformation Kit complete with follow-along workout DVDs, Intervals for Busy Moms with soundtracks and follow-along videos as well as a Fit Yummy Mummy Cookbook.

She is also the founder of ClubFYM.com ~ The Best Online Support Community for Moms. Moms meet online to get connected, feel supported and successfully transform their bodies by taking part in Transformation Challenges, personally interacting with Holly and receiving 2 new fat-burning workouts each month with follow-along videos.

Holly graduated from the University of Louisville with a Masters of Arts in Teaching. She has worked with over 11,000 Mom's to help them lose the stubborn baby fat and get and even better pre-baby body back. As a trainer, friend and coach, it is Holly's mission to educate, motivate and inspire women to take action and go after their dreams and goals.

For more information about Holly and the fat-loss programs and support she has to offer, plus grab a free Get Your Body Back Starter Pack, visit her blog at: www.GetFitAndYummy.com
or send an email to: Holly@FitYummyMummy.com

CHAPTER 12

13 MINDSET PRINCIPLES OF A CHAMPION

BY ANTHONY INCOLLINGO

Consistency and persistence can lead to the life of a champion, whether it be in the classroom, in the gym or in everyday life; champions are built on taking risks, understanding rewards and being prepared if failure comes along the way. Take a moment to reflect on where you are at in your own life? Are you happy? Could you change the way of your thinking? Are there things about yourself that you are willing to change? Are there things that you would like to accomplish? If you are answering these questions, I have piqued your curiosity and now have you engaged and interested in what it takes to develop a "champion mindset." If developed and constantly applied, the principles I will outline can lead you to achieve your own life-altering experiences.

First, lets take a look at a couple of scenarios. The following scenarios are samples of everyday people and some of the issues they may face. Whether you are trying to succeed in the business world, reach the pinnacle of athleticism or conquer weight-loss goals, challenges will arise and obstacles will set you back. However, no matter where your journey begins and how you respond to adversity, each individual can become his or her own champion.

For years Cindy had battled with her addiction to food by allowing it to consume her life. Food was comfort for Cindy and after numerous attempts with fad diets, weight loss pills and even trying to starve her way to success, Cindy seemed to fail along the way until one day, she decided enough was enough. Cindy started her weight-loss journey weighing in at an astounding weight of 305 pounds. Throughout her journey, Cindy faced challenges such as diabetes, high blood pressure and even cardiac problems. These issues caused many problems in Cindy's life, such as turmoil with her children, husband and even coworkers. Cindy realized that the core issue here was her significant weight gain.

Not being comfortable in her own skin, Cindy distanced herself from her peers, family and career. The motivation and will power in Cindy's demeanor was certainly there so it was difficult to understand why success did not follow. Upon further review of her lifestyle and mental outlook on attaining her goals, I realized she lacked the guidance and direction needed to overcome her food addiction. After providing her with the 13 Principles of a "Champion Mindset" I witnessed a change in Cindy's attitude towards herself. She began to adopt the principles I set forth and found success by reaching milestones that she could not before. Six months into her new mindset, Cindy had made tremendous progress not only with weight-loss but also psychologically, gaining confidence and will power to continue on her journey. Cindy reached her final weight-loss goal within 2 years, and continues to strive emotionally, physically and mentally due to having a "champion mindset."

Joe, an undefeated wrestler during his regular season, seems to always choke under the pressure of the big arena with the championship on the line. Joe is 'above and beyond' committed to his sport. He spends countless hours in the gym, on the mats and working with professionals, to develop wrestling techniques that are beyond his years of experience. Joe is physically fit, fast and powerful. He has all of the physical attributes that would make the average wrestler fearful to face him in competition. However, Joe did not emphasize some of the 13 Principles of a "Champion Mindset" – instead putting them on the back burner behind his physical training. Joe was not informed that a stellar athlete needs more then a fixed mindset of being physically fit and encompassing sound technique.

While competing during a dual meet schedule, Joe's coach noticed a significant difference between the champion wrestlers and Joe – based solely upon their way of thinking during key pressure situations. Joe's coach reached out to me to assist in instilling the fundamental principles of a "champion mindset." These principles allowed Joe new levels of success during his training, which helped him to better prepare for top-level competition. This mindset was not easily instilled into Joe seeing as it took years to build up a poor mental outlook on what mental success is. With dedication to changing his ways, I was able to help him slowly develop a new mindset that he incorporated into his daily life. By adopting this "Champion Mindset" in the early phase of his high school career, he was able to fully believe that he was a true champion physically, mentally and emotionally. Throughout the duration of his high school wrestling career, Joe steadily improved and excelled, becoming a top-notch wrestler at the state and national level. By his senior year, he was a nationally-ranked wrestler and went on to become a college All-American.

In the two scenarios that you just read, there is evidence to support that "champion mindset" principles can be learned and incorporated into your daily life and putting you on the path to success. Throughout my lifelong involvement in sport as an athlete, parent, teacher and coach, I have witnessed firsthand the necessities needed for physical and mental performance in athletes. The last 27 years of my life have been dedicated to developing a pliable and attainable mindset, in addition to the physical development that is needed to foster a successful environment among various types of clients (including but not limited to athletes, those struggling with weight-loss and your weekend warrior). These people are all looking to gain knowledge and insight into their own personal health and wellbeing as they embark on their individual journeys.

From my interactions with athletes, coaches and clients I have found a need to encourage the "Champion Mindset" Principles on a daily basis in order to obtain the results they want in their lives. Daily stressors and hardships are only limiting factors on each individual and can be *reduced* if the 13 "Champion Mindset" Principles are applied. I developed a way for my clients to focus and find a style to cope with all that life is throwing at them. These beliefs and methods provide them with the opportunity to enhance and achieve a high level of optimal performance, not limited to physical and mental potential.

Listed below are the 13 "Champion Mindset" Principles suggested to enhance optimal growth, power and success in any aspect of your life:

1. *Write your goals down* - Seeing your goals in your face constantly will reassure you that you are on your way to success. It is the first thing you should look at when you wake up and the last thing you should see before you retire in the evening. GOALS, GOALS, GOALS!!! Remind yourself daily of what you are fighting for; short term and long term goals are constantly evolving to suit your specific needs.

2. *Courage* - Be aware of your self-worth by understanding your value. Do not be afraid to take risks and embrace failure by understanding it. You are stronger than you believe and wiser than you think. Do not let setbacks keep you from getting up again.

3. *Perseverance* - When things are not going your way, a champion has the diligence to fight through, battle back, embrace the grind and make a comeback.

4. *Focus* - This may be the most obvious one on the list but being obvious does not always make it easy to follow and stay on task. Concentrate on what your goal is and refocus if you get off track.

5. *Power of Positivity* - Finding the good in all situations, not allowing your mind to wander and breed negativity, constantly thinking about the good that has happened or will happen. By remaining optimistic you will see the glass half-full instead of half-empty and allow the possibilities of your goals to be limitless.

6. *Motivation* - Whom are you doing this for? What gives you the fire in your belly? Where do you seek inspiration and drive? When will you start? Why are you ultimately doing this? How will you keep going? Only you can answer these questions, only you have the answers.

7. *Visualize* - Close your eyes and imagine the feeling of becoming a prosperous champion in whatever you want to succeed. Hear the crowd cheer you on; feel your heart pounding as adrenaline pushes you forward; embrace the end result. Find the moment that you have been striving for – become a champion! Paint a picture in your mind of the before and after and see yourself at the finish line.

8. *Ownership* - Take accountability for your own actions. Be diligent and responsible for the steps you take to reach new heights. You cannot change how people will act, what they will say or what they will do, but you can control how you react after disappointment(s).

9. *Reflection* - Give yourself the time, chance and ability to look back, analyze and improve upon. Adapt and overcome by having the will to change.

10. *Precision* - Follow all of the steps and resources given to you including the materials and learning tools. The key to real success is having no room for error, the more detailed you are. . . the more successful you will be.

11. *Mental Toughness* - How tough are you? Are you willing to break out of your comfort zone? By developing the ability to outsmart your opposition (which includes yourself) you will be better prepared in your mental state to follow your physical demands. Your opponent does not have to be a physical being, it could be a demon within. Stay strong always.

12. *Fear/Nervousness* - Butterflies and fear of your opponent are good. These feelings reassure your focus, drive and dedication to becoming a champion. Never put yourself on a pedestal, that is the easiest way to get knocked down.

13. *Pleasure/Enjoyment* - What is the underlying meaning for you to becoming successful? You must want whatever you desire for yourself first and foremost. And although the road to victory will be difficult, you must love the process of becoming your best self.

Although I have outlined these 13 "Champion Mindset" Principles for you to follow, these ideologies do not always fall in numerical order. They can also be repeated during any period of time in order to achieve your end result. A "Champion Mindset" will never rest; there is always room to grow, improve, learn and develop your own principles to add to your repertoire. A champion is someone who dedicates himself or herself to physically train day-in and day-out. By mastering technique, following vigorous strengthening and conditioning protocols and adhering to sound nutritional advice, one can only take themselves so far. Training needs to go beyond the realm of physicality. Champions mentally train every second of the day. The art of combining the physical, nutritional, emotional and most importantly, the mental together, creates an unstoppable synergy. By incorporating these 13 "Champion Mindset" Principles into your life, you too can be one step closer to finding the champion in you!

About Anthony

Anthony Incollingo is the President/Owner of Speed Pursuit, LLC, the premiere strength and conditioning facility in Southeastern Pennsylvania. He also serves as Health/Physical Education Teacher, Co-Chairperson in the Health and Physical Education Department in the Pennsbury School District and is a varsity wrestling coach in the Neshaminy School District.

Anthony holds a Master's Degree in Exercise Science from California University of Pennsylvania and a Bachelor's Degree in Health and Physical Education from The College of New Jersey. He is a Performance Enhancement Specialist with the National Academy of Sports Medicine, Sports Performance Coach with USA Weightlifting, a Youth Fitness Specialist and holds many specialty certifications including Metabolic Training Expert, Kettlebell Coach, Resistance Band Training Specialist, Core Conditioning Specialist, Mixed Marshal Arts Conditioning, Underground Strength Coach and much more.

Anthony has been helping athletes move to the next level since 2001. He has an impressive client list which includes NHL Draft Picks, professional athletes and NCAA Division I, II and III athletes. He has a passion for working with student athletes and developing them so they have the ability to compete at the highest levels. He also runs highly successful fitness boot camps and classes for working adults and helps them transform and reach their fitness goals.

Anthony is a panel fitness expert in the *Training Edge Magazine* and has written articles for several fitness publications. Anthony was nominated and entered into the running for the 2015 International Youth Conditioning Association Coach of the Year Award. His gym motto is "We Build Champions" and he truly believes that through hard work, anyone can be a "Champion" in the gym, classroom, playing field or life!

You can connect with Anthony at:
Speedpursuit@comcast.net
www.facebook.com/Speed.Pursuit

Speed Pursuit, LLC.
160 Bordentown Road
Tullytown, PA 19007
215-946-2372

CHAPTER 13

REALISM FOR FITNESS

BY DUSTIN WILLIAMS

A client came to me one day after hitting rock bottom in her life. She had gained weight from two childbirths, couldn't manage to maintain a workout routine, was feeling unattractive for her husband, and was on the brink of an emotional breakdown. Although I couldn't relate to her on a number of the issues going on in her life, I was able to share in the frustrations of being overweight and feeling out of control of my body. I told her my struggles with weight after going through college and joining the corporate world and how a breakup with a girlfriend had kicked me back into the love of fitness. From personal experience and continued stories of similar women and men coming to me, I was able to guide her through the beginning mental and emotional steps of succeeding towards her lifestyle change.

For many people, the thought of transforming your life into a lifestyle of health and happiness seems overwhelming and taking those first steps seems impossible. Once you have decided a change is necessary, you may find yourself hitting a roadblock for the next step. The advice I gave to my emotionally and physically disgruntled client will be the same advice for you as a reader. It will help you begin your journey, maintain a positive outlook during times of high stress, and boost your self-esteem as you learn to master positive comparison.

CREATE GOALS

Taking the first step towards a 'new you' requires not only the mindset of dedication, but a plan of action to make sure you realistically set yourself up for success. Sitting down beforehand and creating a list of goals can help you get started towards the end results you would like to see. Whether you want to be lean, increase your endurance, or pack on muscle weight, a game plan is necessary from day one.

An important component in the creation of a goal is reality. Take a look at your current lifestyle, the resources you have around you, and the current quality of health you hold. Perhaps you have struggled with high blood pressure medications or the doctors have warned you about the dangers of your cholesterol numbers crawling upwards on the scale. Throughout my family history, diabetes and hypertension have caused drastic problems in the health of my loved ones. As I have grown older, I've seen my grandfather have three open-heart surgeries and witnessed my uncle's gradual loss of vision from diabetes. With this knowledge, I've been able to prepare my mind and body to overcome those obstacles in life and rearrange my goals to reject the health issues that have plagued my family. Realizing the chaos of your own current lifestyle and how you can change the surrounding variables are vital in the goal-creating process. If you take the time to write down these issues that surround your lifestyle, you will be more apt to take the steps in improving these areas of your life.

In addition to recognizing the issues with your health and lifestyle, pinpoint the areas of significance and discover what matters to you in your transformation. Many times, people change because they'd like to take a more active role in their children's lives, they would like to win the admiration of the opposite sex, or release themselves from the health advisories doctors impose. Although it is helpful to be specific in the goal process, such as having a weight of 120 pounds or decreasing your waist size by 4 inches, it is more important to recognize areas of your life that will be impacted throughout your transformation. During times of setbacks or high stress, leaning against those surroundings areas, not just the numbers your scale or tape measure reflects, will provide you encouragement as you go through your goals. If you have a rough week of sticking to your diet plan and your scale goes up by two pounds, having the ability to keep up with your running toddler, a task you may have not been able to do before, will be more significant than the numbers you have gained.

Once you have established a plan of action, the task of completing it is ahead of you. Keeping reality in mind, ask yourself what is step one? What type of diet do you need to get to your goal? How many times do you need to workout per week? Do you need to hire a personal trainer? By confronting yourself with these questions, you're taking the first step in reaching your goal. From the list you previously developed of health issues and the environment you currently live in, sift out the questions that individualize your personal workout routine and diet plan. If you're a diabetic, you should be aware of the foods you can or cannot have; therefore, your diet plan will be different, as you have to maintain your insulin levels as you are exercising. If you happen to be vegan, your plan needs to include a vast variety of proteins as you workout, but it will be a different diet plan to another person who chooses to eat animal products. By forcing yourself into the mindset that you must answer these questions for success, you will move into the next stage of your new life.

After you have done the footwork in the creation of your goals, you may find it wearisome to look at it knowing all of the cardio, weight lifting, sweating, and dieting that is to come. However, do not let yourself down at this point. You are in control of your own lifestyle, happiness, and health. To lay out the foundation of your new life will be futile if you do not attempt to carry out the plan. Most people can identify the areas of their body and life they'd like to improve, but they usually lack the motivation to stick to their plan. Grab a friend, an iPod, your child, your dog, a new workout outfit, or whatever it may be to help get you motivated and go get started!

THE DANGERS OF USING NEGATIVITY IN DIETING

The groans and whines of dieters can be heard all over society. Walking in the mall, going to the gym, shopping at the supermarket, or at the local diner, the timeless "I'm on a diet" accompanied by a throaty moan can be heard. The stigma that is attached to dieting is not a reputation anyone would like to have: awful, inconvenient, unsatisfying, time consuming, costly, and many times unsuccessful. From the moment a person can grasp the concept of a diet, they are surrounded by diets that their moms, aunts, dads, cousins, best friends, or celebrity icons promote. From the grapefruit diet, no carbohydrate diet, extreme low calorie diet, to the HCG diet, the list of diets to choose from is exhausting. However, what is more exhausting than choosing a diet is battling the inner desire to repel all diets because of the shame and struggle that comes with the limitations.

Much like transforming your outer appearance, the transformation during this time of your life needs to also occur within your mind. Attaching the negativity that comes with dieting will only create havoc within the game plan you've set up for yourself. Remind yourself as you're going through your dieting and exercise routine, that you've created success for yourself through these steps. This process of reprogramming your mind to function on positivity requires continual regrouping back to your goals to keep the motivation level up. Once you can start associating dieting and exercising with the positivity it will bring to your life, such as the pleasure of losing fat, gaining muscle, a physique appealing to the opposite sex, or winning your competition, you will find more pleasure in the world of fitness.

YOU CAN'T CREATE THE PERFECT MEAL PLAN

The world would be a much simpler place if you could pull up to your local fast food restaurant, glance at the menu to the area your diet is found, and place a quick order of High Protein Punch and Lean Lentil Lunch. However, the world of fast food has not evolved as fast as the fitness world would like it to, and your diet is not going to be as convenient as you'd like it to be. You're going to face challenges and obstacles as you face your days of clean eating, but keep in mind the importance of changing your lifestyle rather than jumping on a 12 week binge on fruits and veggies only to jump into a bread bowl on week 13. You've already recognized the need for an individualized diet; our bodies are all wired differently, so the metabolism of one person will not necessarily support a diet another person has flourished on. With this being understood, it's also vital for you to understand that you cannot create the perfect meal plan.

Frequently, people come into my gym and they've tried the fad diets, they've lost weight, they've gained weight, and they cannot figure out why they cannot keep the weight off. With one simple question, I'm able to understand what the underlying issue is: "Have you made a lifestyle change?" A stint of a couple weeks on a diet is not a lifestyle change, it is simply a quick fix that ultimately sends your body into confusion as you plunge it back into your previous lifestyle of unhealthy eating. With the endless resources provided today- your doctor, the internet, television, the library, your trainer- you should be able to gain enough knowledge on eating healthy without limiting yourself to the point of exhaustion or to the point of relapse, which frequently occurs on these types of diets.

To keep yourself focused and not get overwhelmed with the numbers and figures, keep your diet simple. Simplicity will help make your diet easier to follow and allow you to make detours during times when you may not be able to 'scarf down' the healthy foods you had planned. The most helpful tip I can provide you with for success in your new diet is doing your research to become knowledgeable in what foods will boost your metabolism, what foods will complement each other well in building muscle mass, and what foods are healthy additions to your everyday life no matter what diet you are on. Using the resources that are available to you will only provide you with more motivation to reach your goal.

DON'T SET YOURSELF UP FOR DISAPPOINTMENT

Most people that come into my gym can reminisce about the days when they were in high school and wearing a size two in pants, but they come in with the realistic goal of fat loss or muscle gain. Being able to identity a safe and manageable goal in your weight will also be a reflection of the happiness and satisfaction you will receive once you complete that goal. By creating an impractical idea of what you would like yourself to look like after a month or six weeks or by next year, you're automatically setting yourself up for failure and relapse when you are unable to reach that goal.

When you decide to lose fat and get your life on the right track, you usually make this over a short period of time. Whilst doing so, you forget that it took months or even a matter of years to put the weight on. Even though you may begin to see changes over a short period of time, the dramatic recreation of yourself could take just as long as it did to put on that weight. By revisiting the goals and significant areas of your life previously discussed, you will be able to make your way through those times of stress and relapse as you receive encouragement from how far you've managed to come.

Following the common denominator of the lifestyle change, it's important to realize that fat loss and having an amazing physique is a commitment. The best guys in the industry have taken the time to figure out how to stay consistent in the long haul. By being realistic on the fat loss possible and the sacrifices you're willing to take, you will be able to set yourself up for success in a long-term setting.

BIRDS OF A FEATHER FLOCK TOGETHER

Growing up in a tight-knit family, I have always found pleasure in the Sunday afternoons spent at my grandmother's house. Even now, thinking about her homemade foods, all fried and packed with calories, makes my mouth water. We would spend hours surrounding the table, exchanging memories and stories of the week, while soaking up the good food she had worked hard to prepare. Even though these special family moments were significant in my childhood and teen years, I knew I had to make a change to make it to my goals.

After explaining to my family that I would be making some sacrifices and developing a healthier way of living, my family was supportive and not offended when I chose to find interventions while with them. Instead of filling up on my grandmother's unhealthy foods, I'd have a small healthy meal beforehand and go to her house afterwards for the socialization. Even though this wasn't the most convenient- or enjoyable- option, it helped keep me on track with my fat loss goals.

Because I had also voiced my goals and plan to my family, they kept me accountable and supported me when I had moments of weakness.

Much like my experience with my family, you have people in your life that you can identify as destructive to your fat loss goals. Whether it is family or friends, you must voice your new lifestyle change to them and request their support as you will hit challenges along the way. If you have found yourself in a lifestyle rut of drinking late with your friends, sleeping in until noon, and missing the first few meals of the day, you're setting yourself up for failure from the beginning. By bringing your friends and family on board, you're able to create a motivational army to help you towards those goals rather than hinder you. Instead of staying out late with the guys every night, start with limiting yourself to two nights a week while encouraging a less unhealthy activity for the remaining nights of the week. Your lifestyle and the encouragement you receive from your peers will be an integral component of your fitness journey.

With your outer appearance changing, your diet fulfilling your nutritional needs, and toxins being worked out of your body, you will find your mind will become clearer to realize the negativity that you have surrounded yourself within certain friends or family members. By surrounding yourself with like-minded people, people wishing to succeed in their goals and become healthier individuals, you will feel empowered and encouraged to continue on.

THERE IS MORE TO FITNESS THAN GENETICS

Whenever I made the decision to start exercising and get healthy, I walked into my local gym and was immediately intimidated by high school students lifting much more than I could at that time. Although I felt embarrassed and overwhelmed to begin with, I comforted myself with the simple truth that everyone has a starting point. Not everyone could walk into the gym and bench 300 pounds; only with dedication and a plan of action could someone train to get to that point.

When you see a guy who has a ripped physique, it's not productive to think to yourself

"I've not been blessed with those genetics" or "I'll never look that great!" Quick-fired thoughts like that cause you to forget the sacrifices that he's made and the consistency he's kept in his schedule. Instead of turning the situation into a negative and hindering yourself in your workout, use that image of the physique you'd like to have as motivation. Comparisons can cause you to step up your game and get out of your comfort zone.

Your perception of yourself is the key element in how much you can or can't compare yourself to others. If you find yourself judging your body by comparing it to those around you, you will be neglecting the goals and significant areas of your changing life. For instance, you may not have the physique of the woman that has been training for three more months than you, but you have been taken off your of high cholesterol medication. Keeping your mind set on these "bigger picture goals" will continue to help you throughout your journey.

The journey you will go on as you reach your goals will be a time of inner and outer transformation. By keeping your mind focused on the positivity that will be introduced into your life, you will be able to climb over the obstacles that will impede your journey. The knowledge you will gain during this time will be vital to the success of your fitness program and having those other key elements, such as like-minded social groups and a simple meal plan, will keep you focused. My client that came to me with so much negativity and overwhelming issues used this simple format to build herself up into a strong individual; she not only gained muscle mass and admiration of her peers, but she gained a mind full of confidence, endurance, and the ability to look at her progress and feel accomplished. Just like this client, following this setup will provide you with the tools to excel in your fitness journey.

About Dustin

Dustin Williams is the Owner and Head Personal Trainer for Precision Fitness. He has been involved in the fitness world for over eleven years. He began training prior to going to Northeastern State University, where he received a Bachelor's Degree in Finance. After he graduated and began work in the corporate setting, Dustin lost focus on health and wellness - which in turn caused him to gain 40+ pounds. He realized he not only needed to change his habits, but that he also couldn't imagine not helping others to do the same. He went back to school and received both his IBFA certification and is an NSCA Certified Strength & Conditioning Specialist. Now he has lost 50 pounds and continues to focus on his nutritional education and knowledge. He has attended one of the most prestigious boot camp training sessions in Las Vegas, and has also trained with four-time Mr. Olympia, Jay Cutler. Dustin has currently been training clients full-time for over 5 years, and has helped many lose weight, gain muscle, and achieve their goals. People know Dustin as a focused individual and that he is someone who will help them achieve their goals...no matter what it takes. In addition to personal training, Dustin also currently is the Regional Head Judge for Natural Bodybuilding competitions.

Precision Fitness is North West Arkansas's Premier Fitness Boot Camp for men AND women of all walks of life and delivers the best Personal Training in the area! It serves to help Bentonville residents look and feel better than ever with 30-Minute EXPRESS group metabolic workouts for busy men AND women! Precision Fitness is also a member of the Fitness Revolution Franchise.

To Connect with Dustin:
(479) 273-5707
Facebook.com/dustin.k.williams
Facebook.com/precisionfitnessnwa
http://www.PrecisionFitnessNWA.com

CHAPTER 14

HOW TO DESIGN 'GUARANTEED RESULTS' TRAINING PROGRAMS

BY JON LeTOCQ

When I first qualified as a trainer, I worked at the typical chrome-plated leisure club that looked like an Egyptian bazaar where members chose what ever took their fancy each day. The concept of following a set program that would DEFINITELY produce results, was deemed 'unnecessary' by many.

One day I approached a middle-aged guy on the 'pec dec' with a super- size spare tyre. I suggested a few changes to his program and got a reply I will never forget.

"Thanks son, but I've been doing the same program for nine years, so I don't need all your new fancy stuff."

NINE YEARS IN THE GYM AND STILL FAT!

I wish I could say this was a rare occurrence, but it's now a rarity to find someone who HAS got the body they want. I had to get out and work with people who genuinely want to see change, be the change and not just be entertained with TV's and lycra.

I'm still learning and always will be, but with more and more people qualifying as gym instructors and personal trainers, yet rapidly increasing rates of obesity and ill health, I can categorically state one thing: Most of the industry is getting it seriously wrong in attempts to just entertain or sell stuff.

Having worked with a professional rugby player, Guernsey First XV Rugby, Guernsey Cricket, numerous amateur athletes, a lady who went from 20 stone* 10 to 10 stone 5, nurses, GP's, office workers, lawyers, under 18's, mums and just about every profession you can imagine, I've seen a few things work, but many more fail. The catch is that some programs can be guaranteed to work for some people, but not others.

Here's what I know so far…

BALANCED PROGRAMS

Guaranteed results programs don't look at balance in terms of working opposing muscles the same – but aligning where you are now with where you want to be.

Desk Jockey Dave is a round-shouldered office worker. Performing equal numbers of sets and reps on his chest and upper back will simply make him bigger or at least stronger in the same poor position. His risk of shoulder injury or back problems will not improve and will most likely get worse unless he starts to work more on his back than on his chest to address the existing imbalance.

Desk Jockey Dave's glute muscles are also likely to be suffering from some kind of dysfunction due to sitting down all day. He thinks he is doing the right thing by doing lots of squats, dead lifts and lunges for a 'balanced' workout, but in fact he is overloading those muscles which have to compensate for glute weakness, in particular his lower back. This is made worse in the presence of poor ankle or hip mobility.

At the other end of the spectrum, focusing all your efforts correcting the posture of a rugby player or cyclist, can in fact DETRACT from their performance. In the grand scheme of life it may help these people to improve their posture, but in terms of their sport, performance may

---

* A stone is an Imperial unit of weight equal to 14 avoirdupois pounds (6.35029318 kg).

well drop because their body has adapted to an optimal position for their sport which you are now trying to breakdown.

What's optimal for elite sport, fast muscle gain or movie star fat loss, isn't always optimal for health and vice-versa. Whilst health should feature heavily in all programs, there is a need to switch between methods if particular goals are required…and fast.

"If all you have is a hammer, every thing begins to look like a nail."

Don't try to create a program based on entertainment – you can't guarantee results that way. For instance, if you want to complete a sub 1 hours print triathlon, don't do 2-3 hours per week 'pumping the guns' or doing torturous 1 hour conditioning sessions.

Be specific. Every session and every exercise moves you closer to, or further away from, your goal.

MAKE ROOM FOR SUCCESS

Is there room in your life for the Guaranteed Results program? If it is impossible to fit it in with your responsibilities as a parent, employee or business owner, the program will fall flat.

Sacrifices need to be made to be successful in anything, but they also need to 'fit' certain other criteria.

HOW TO MAKE THE PROGRAM FIT

Health and fitness programming has become about how many sets and reps are required for strength versus power; endurance versus muscle growth. It seems so long as we get these right, we know we're in the ballpark for good results.

Unfortunately, these factors are sometimes the LAST piece of the jigsaw – particularly outside of the elite sport world where training and competition is often the only concern.

Take Desk Jockey Dave.

His mate has stacked on 10kg of muscle in six months, training six times each week. Dave fancies a piece of the action since seeing his muscular body disappear when the kids arrived on the scene...

He tries the program for two weeks then finds his muscles ache all the time, he's falling asleep at work and he's put on virtually no muscle.

Now, Dave and his wife have two kids to run around after on top of his stressful finance job, and his levels of the stress hormone cortisol are through the roof. Cortisol is affected by chronic stress levels and not only does it have a catabolic affect on muscle tissue, but it also creates systemic inflammation, greatly affecting recovery. The program is now just piling more stress on to Dave's body and mind and dragging him down further.

Dave's wife Caroline is also failing to see any results at her new Intense Bootcamp combined with a high protein, low fat, low carb diet, even though it did wonders for her friend. No matter how hard Caroline tries, the weight won't shift, so she cuts more calories. Now she's tired all the time and gets severe hunger cravings resulting in Saturday night binges. She's actually putting on weight!

Again, the reason is that the program is not right for CAROLINE. It works for her friend who can relax by the pool and have a sauna whilst Caroline tears her hair out running around after the kids.

Caroline is also a serial dieter. Every diet she has done has further disrupted her hormones including her insulin (controls blood sugar) and leptin (controls hunger and appetite).

In between crazy starvation diets, Caroline binges and eats lots of bad food, so her digestive system is clogged up with processed food and high levels of meat – dragging her energy levels down even more. Leptin is no longer produced properly in Caroline, so she doesn't get the proper "I'm full" signals, hence the constant hunger pangs.

Her adrenal glands are also malfunctioning, unable to keep producing high levels of adrenaline to cope with all the daily stresses and challenges. So the bootcamp which SHOULD bring fat loss doesn't work for Caroline. She doesn't have the energy to train hard, and the high protein diet isn't helping because it's dragging her energy levels down even further.

What should Caroline do?

Cardio, Weights, Aerobic Exercise or High Intensity Interval Training?

There are so many ways to train it can look like a minefield! Go on the internet and you'll see people arguing over long-steady cardio, intervals or no cardio. Some favour heavy strength training for joint and ligament health as well as muscle gain, whereas others never go near weights for fear of 'bulking up'.

The truth is that ALL of the different modes have incredible value in guaranteeing results in certain situations. The key to programming the min requires looking at the individual's goals and their current stress levels, fitness levels,time availability and body type.

For instance, metabolic conditioning with kettlebells, ropes and tyre-flipping is a fantastic way to increase work capacity, burn body fat and rapidly increase stamina levels FOR SOME PEOPLE. However, for a stressed-out office worker and single Mum of three, it may be the straw that broke the camel's back.

When an individual's 'stress bucket' starts to brim over, it can manifest itself as backache, depression, weight-gain, illness or mood swings. In this case, the best choice would be a relaxation program including some deep breathing or yoga, mind-awareness coaching and light aerobic cardio program which gets the individual out in the open air and oxygenates their blood. The emotional freedom associated with running can make an instant difference to mood and hormones, greatly improving the chances of success.

The cardio work could involve some basic body weight movement patterns, but in such a way that doesn't involve working to failure or stress. Lets assume Caroline can perform 10 good repetitions of body weight squats, push-ups and reverse lunges. A good way to start training would be performing 5 sets of 5 reps of each exercise to introduce movement and training principles without smashing her into the floor!

At first, I wouldn't even time any runs or measure distances. Just let Caroline have some fun and leave with a feeling of progress and accomplishment. Use some boxing to de-stress and get a good sweat on. Caroline should not be attempting to become the next Miss Cross Fit 2011 just yet!

THE FANTASTIC FOUR FOR HIGHLY-STRESSED PEOPLE

If you are permanently stressed, you should look to optimize…

1 - Oxygenation

2 - Perspiration

3 - Defecation

4 - Urination

Ensure totally clean nutrition, controlling animal protein consumption.

Drink loads of water and schedule some light, relaxing exercise. This will help reset hormones, flush out toxins which drag energy levels down and affect brain performance, improve digestion and optimize metabolic function for fat burning.

The key to program management going forward lies in knowing when to 'up-the-pace', but there is no black and white answer. It takes careful observation.

When you see life come back and a zest for exercise reappear, you can start introducing fitness tests, and bring in some free-weight training, progressing to harder sessions. The session structure is dependent on the goal, not what you like doing!

Be prepared however, to take a step back should life become too stressful again, making it difficult to cope with hardcore training on top.

IF YOU CAN'T GAIN, DON'T TRAIN

You either move forwards or backwards with fitness training–there is no in-between!

The key lies in getting to know yourself and recording your physical and mental reactions to times of stress, methods of training and the results.

Track...

1. Your weight and body fat
2. Performance indices such as your favourite 5k run or weights lifted
3. Your motions and energy levels as the program progresses
4. Your resting heart rate
5. Your blood pressure

These five factors will tell you all you need to know about whether Guaranteed Results are around the corner.

THE GUARANTEED RESULTS PROGRAM

You should have realized by now that recommending one program is like playing 'Pin-The-Tail-On-The-Donkey.' Instead, here are the principles for different goals for you to grasp and apply daily.

In addition to the points below, all categories require adherence to a clean, natural diet, the details of which can't be covered sufficiently here. However, if you only drink 2-3 litres of filtered water eat lean, organic proteins, lots of vegetables, healthy fats and keep starchy carbs to post training meals, you won't be far off!

1. STRESSED OUT BUSY BODY

You need to...

...reset hormones by making time for relaxation, breathing and an absence of technology and sources of stress.

...introduce light aerobic work, which can include body weight exercises and traditional cardio (taking into consideration impact and obesity factors).

...avoid stressful, anaerobic exercise for the first few weeks.

Typical session:

- Movement preparation circuit   15 minutes
- Boxing 5 rounds of 1 min 30 with 1 min 30 light jog to recover
- Dynamic stretching and yoga movements   10 minutes
- Seated deep breathing   10 minutes

2. FAST FAT LOSS (ASSUMING LOW DAILY STRESS LEVELS)

You need...

...full body resistance sessions 3-4 times per week.

...sessions beginning with hypertrophic work and ending with metabolic conditioning work (high intensity, short rest breaks and 'Timed' challenges of 10-15 minutes).

...possibly extra aerobic intervals 2-3 times per week (6-10 x 200-400m @80% of max effort on each interval with walk back or jog back recovery). This may be unnecessary if you are a tall, lean body ectomorphic bodytype.

Typical session:

A1: Overhead press, 3 x 8 reps, 30 seconds rest

A2: Reverse lunge, 3 x 10 reps each side, 30 seconds rest

B1: Step up, 3 x 8 reps each side, 30 seconds rest

B2: Pushups, 3 x 15 reps, 30 seconds rest

Finisher:

As Many Rounds As Possible in 15 minutes...

20 burpees

100m sprint

50 reps on battling ropes

3. MUSCLE BUILDING

This is another area in which one size doesn't fit all.

A boxer may want to gain weight but maintain his lethal, lightning bolt of a right hook – so he should not be performing slow grinding bench presses which reduce his rate of force production. He also won't want to ache so much that he can't lift his arms tomorrow!

A bodybuilding competitor however, may not care how fast he can punch, and slow repetitions may work better for tearing muscle apart ready for being rebuilt bigger.

A rugby player might need more size, and so needs to be packing on muscle and gaining strength for performance.

So we might look at a strength-hypertrophy program (with the focus on hypertrophy) in the off-season, moving to a greater focus on strength and power as we get closer to the start of the nextseason.

In all circumstances, I would always have a Big Bang heavy strength exercise at the start of each session such as squat, deadlift or overhead press followed by non-competing supersets. I would also add some sprints for the athletes.

The method, rep ranges and tempo of lifting would change if we want to guarantee results for all three guys.

Typical upper body session:

A1:Hang clean	5 sets of 5	60 seconds rest
B1:Overhead press	7-9 reps, 3-5 reps, 10-12 reps	
B2: Single arm row	10-12 reps, 6-8 reps, 12-15 reps	
C1: Reverse ab curl	3 sets of 15	30 seconds rest

If you need to shed some fat, finish with 10-15 minutes intense conditioning work such as battling ropes, tyre flips and kettle bell complexes.

There is no need to over-complicate things with twelve different exercises.

Go heavy and go hard on the basics.

GUARANTEED RESULTS

The only way to 'guarantee results' is to get everything spot on for each individual's goals and current physical, emotional and lifestyle status. To do this requires awareness of what's happening day-to-day, week by week and month-on-month.

If you can't do this for yourself, hiring a trainer is essential – otherwise you face years of playing Pin-The-Tail-On-The-Donkey in the gym.

There ARE Guaranteed Results out therefor you, but they don't come in a 'done-for-you' neatly packaged DVD!

About Jon

Jon Le Tocq was voted UK Personal Trainer of the Year 2011 and owns Storm Force Fitness, Guernsey's leading body transformation company.

You know those days when you look great, have loads of energy and feel invincible?

Jon makes that happen.

He and his team of trainers help over 150 people per week achieve their body transformation and sports performance goals – through the Guernsey Fitness Camp, strength and conditioning for teams and exclusive personal training services.

Founding Storm Force Fitness in 009, Jon has rapidly established himself as the 'no nonsense' trainer who inspires his clients and followers to achieve much more than they thought possible, with a talent for pushing the right buttons at the right time.

CHAPTER 15

HOW TO MAKE FITNESS FUN! WELL, BETTER THAN FUN... TRULY REWARDING

BY NIKI DAVIS

Does this title sound like an oxymoron? Does anyone really enjoy exercising? What if I told you fitness could not only be more fun, but it could also be rewarding on so many more levels, inspire you to work harder at your job, your relationships and even be a better parent. Now you really think I am nuts, right? Quite the contrary, I just like to take my clients fitness very seriously and as a career personal trainer, it is important to me that my clients want to exercise not just for the next 10 weeks, but for the rest of their lives.

Let me tell you a story about a lady named Lynn. Lynn came to me about seven years ago after I had worked with her son over the summer between his junior and senior year of high school so that he could make it onto the varsity crew team. He had worked hard all summer and did indeed make it onto the varsity team. Was he having fun during those one-on-one sessions as I worked him harder and harder and with less and less rest and then sent him for a run when we were finished? I would like to think so, but in the moment, I doubt he did. Did he enjoy himself when he was finishing first or second on conditioning runs instead of close to last like in the previous season's tryouts? You bet he did!

Let's get back to Lynn, as I said she came to me that Fall and decided that she would like to start exercising more regularly and thought I could help her get more fit. So we sat down, set some goals and started to exercise. Before long, she was a regular client twice a week with me. But the tide really changed when Lynn decided to take me up on competing in a triathlon in the spring and she joined my beginner triathlon class. We had from that Fall all the way until Mother's Day in May, plenty of time, I assured her, to train for the big day, …and so we began. Now Lynn wasn't just exercising, she was training for an event! Suddenly, she was coming into the gym on days that we weren't scheduled to meet. She was working on her swim, running on the treadmill and meeting our group for bike rides on the weekend. Did I mention that Lynn was at that time mother to three teenagers, on the fundraising board for the crew team, and busy with a million other things that involved taking care of everyone else. But suddenly she was taking 3-4 hours a week to focus on herself.

When Mother's Day came, she was ready. She was a bit nervous, but confident and ready. Lynn finished the triathlon, a women's only event where the tables were turned. For a change, her husband and 3 children were there to support her, cheer her on and had tears in their eyes when she finished. I was so proud of her as she crossed the finish line, as was her family. However, the icing on the cake for me was finding out months later that her teenage daughter had a picture of Lynn, her mother, finishing her triathlon on her computer as a screen saver. Do you think this sent a message to her two daughters?

There is a direct correlation between your physical sense of self and your self-esteem. If you feel more comfortable in your skin, it will show. You will carry yourself differently. Furthermore, they say children get most of their self-esteem from their same-sex parent. So, do we as women want to teach our daughters that once you have children you don't take care of yourself anymore, and just do for everyone else? Do men want to teach their sons physical fitness and sports are only for the youth. …Then on to 60 hour work weeks?

When was the last time you challenged yourself to do something that you really didn't think you could do? I mean physically. Lynn didn't know how to swim properly, hadn't biked in years and never for 12 miles, and

142

running wasn't exactly her favorite pastime. The reason it scares us so much is that we are afraid to fail, but what if you could overcome that fear, ... prepare, train, succeed. I guarantee this new-found success will carry over into other aspects of your life.

Let me tell you something else, I think the more daunting the goal seems to someone, the more the total impact across the board when you realize you can succeed and conquer . Reminding yourself or even learning for the first time that you are stronger than you think, and can push through obstacles and road blocks, can be profound. Then you apply this discovery, this same logic to work, and no job opening is above you, no account too big to handle.

You set goals, get a coach, build a support team, get the right equipment and, one step at a time, you reach those finish lines too. This wasn't an ultimate Ironman that Lynn completed. It was a 1/4 mile swim, 12 mile bike course and 2 mile run, but how many of you think "I could never do that"? Let me tell you, you can, and if you do, you won't be the same after.

I am not saying everyone should be a triathlete, but you should try something new, and through the coming years as you explore exercise you should continue to try new things. Our bodies were built with muscles to be used, and humans were meant to interact. Yet we spend more and more time motionless in seated positions, and less time face-to-face with other people. So, what do you want to do about it?

Below are 9 Keys to workout success and to set the stage for enjoying a rewarding exercise program:

1. **TAKE MEASUREMENTS AND SET GOALS** – Ok, I admit taking measurements doesn't sound like much fun. In fact, this thought is enough to scare some people away from starting at all, but how will you know how far you have come, or when to celebrate your victories if you don't know where you started?. I recommend taking at least body weight, circumference and body fat percentage measurements. If you

haven't exercised in years, I also recommend you go get some blood work done. Again, more for the fun and reward later of seeing how much better your Cholesterol, blood pressure and blood sugar will be, once you are exercising regularly.

Goals are equally important and should be as specific as possible and include a goal date. " I would like to lose twenty pounds by my 35th birthday, May 29, 2011" is much more powerful and likely to be met than a vague goal like, "I would like to lose some weight" or "I would like to tone up." What exactly does that mean? How much weight? By when? How do you know when you have reached "tone up"? Ideally, set and re-evaluate these goals at least quarterly, so every three months you have goals to focus on. I usually have my clients set 3 different types of goals.

- **End Result Goals** – This is the one people usually have no trouble coming up with. "I want to lose 20 pounds", "I want to wear a size 6" for women or "I want to fit back into size 36 pants" for men.

- **Process Goals** – This is where most people miss setting a goal. The Process should be a separate goal. How do you plan to accomplish the End Result goal? "I am going to exercise 4-6 days a week for the next 3 months", "I am going to stop drinking Soda/start eating breakfast", and "I will take a yoga class each week to work on my flexibility and help reduce stress."

- **Performance Goals** – Fitness isn't just about weight or pants size. So, this goal only has to do with performance:
  - "I would like to run a mile without stopping."
  - "I would like to do 12 pushups from my toes."
  - "I would like to learn to rollerblade/swim/rock climb."

2. **TAKE A FRIEND OR MAKE A FRIEND** – You set your goals, and hopefully posted them where you can see them regularly, but that doesn't make training toward them fun. What

about those mornings when you plan on going for a run but it's cold outside and sleeping in sounds sooooooo good. If you have a friend that you are meeting you will get up and go. If you are going to cycling class and know your classmates will wonder where you were, you will get up and go. Get to know other people at your gym, join a running club or inspire your friends or coworkers to start exercising with you. Go for a bike ride/ try a dance class together/ sign up for adult swim lessons and then go for coffee or a smoothie instead of just meeting for another high calorie lunch.

3. **GET OUT OF YOUR COMFORT ZONE. EVEN LAUGH AT YOURSELF** – If you want to have fun you have to try something new and maybe even feel a little uncomfortable. I am not a dancer but I have taken the Zumba, a Latin dance class at my gym, I felt a little silly and uncoordinated but I had fun. When I took Group Kick, our version of a Kick Boxing class, I really felt strong and like I could "kick some butt", but I think the only butt that was kicked was mine – from all those kicks and jumps in class. Trying new things will spice up your exercise and help it to be anything but routine, and you might just find that you really enjoy doing something you hadn't expected.

4. **COMPETE!** – 5K, triathlon, dodge ball, basketball league. It doesn't matter if you were formerly an athlete or not. Some of us really thrive on competition, and tapping into this can make the difference to a lasting exercise regimen. Competing with others in your age group or competing to beat yourself can serve as serious motivation. One year my fitness goal was to beat the time of the only 1/2 marathon I had completed before having my two boys. I did it, it was my little competition with my former self to prove to no one but myself that I was as fit as I had been before I had the kids, and it felt great!

5. **TRAIN VS. EXERCISE** – Just like Lynn, when you are training for something, your workouts have direction. You no longer wander aimlessly into the gym just to see what cardio machines

are open. If you are training for a marathon, you are usually running at least three days a week with longer progressive runs once a week. There is no guessing, you are following a training regimen. Bonus, the event itself serves as the end date of your goal.

6. **BE A PART OF SOMETHING BIGGER THAN YOURSELF** – Sign up for an event that raises money for a cause. Check out: www.teamintraining.com, www.nationalmssociety. org, www.tour.diabetes.org or www.avonwalk.org to name only a few. There are a myriad events out there, catering to from first timers to elite athletes, that not only include team training and coaching, but keep you inspired – as you train with and for people who need your support. Many of these events are not races either, so if competing doesn't appeal to you, try the Avon walk for breast cancer or the 2-day 150 mile bike ride for Muscular Sclerosis. Also, many companies will match fundraising, so check with your employer and see if they have a matching program. Then gather some coworkers together for some true team building!

7. **Move every day** – give yourself credit for increasing even your non-exercise activity. Wear a pedometer! This is a great experiment and an easy thing to start. Buy yourself a pedometer and track how many steps you take per day. I work on my feet and on a typical workday, before I do any exercise for myself, I take between 12,000-15,000 steps. However, I have a client that tele-commutes and works from home on a computer. I was shocked to find out that on a day that he doesn't exercise he was regularly logging only 1,000-1,800 steps per day. I couldn't believe it! This kind of inactivity can stall even the best efforts to get in shape. The American Heart Association recommends 10,000 steps a day. Research shows that the average American takes 2,000-5,000 "lifestyle steps", just going about their regular day. By adding just 30 minutes of walking or jogging per day you can raise this number to 10,000 steps. I wore a pedometer consistently for months because of a program we had at work,

and you might be surprised how simple yet motivating and telling it is to see the actual #'s every day. Then when you realize that we can all be extremely inactive at times, you might find yourself washing your own car, walking the dog a little further, or playing tag with the kids instead of just watching.

Every step counts!

8. HIRE A PROFESSIONAL! – Many people think that trainers only have clients that see them 2-3 times a week. Take it from me, yes, I have those clients but I also have some clients I see once a month, once a quarter or every once in a while. If you are ready to take your training to the next level treat yourself to a personal training session every once in a while. If I have someone I know is seeing me to set up a workout plan that they can carry out on their own, I approach the sessions a little differently. I try to educate them on why I put certain exercises in the program by explaining concepts and specific exercise form concerns. I use the fantasy football analogy often, if you were making your own team, you would research credentials, hire proven coaches and recruit quality teammates. The same is true here, find a trainer, nutritionist and support team that will ensure your success.

9. SPEAK POSITIVELY ABOUT EXERCISE – This might sound silly to some, but if you dread exercise or look at it as a punishment for over-indulgence, then of course it isn't going to be fun. Change your internal feelings and dialog about exercise: "I am going to take the 6:00 pm Yoga class on Fridays because it always helps me decompress after a long work week."; "I feel so much stronger since I have been lifting weights."; "Fall is such a beautiful time to go out and hike." This small change can have a big impact on how we view and think about exercise. Try it!

Set Goals, Track your progress, build your team, train for an event, and succeed! Get in touch with your physical self and start to enjoy exercising maybe for the first time in a long time, or for the first time ever!

About Niki

- BS-University of Florida-Exercise and Sport Sciences

- NASM-Performance Enhancement Specialist and Certification Instructor

- NSCA-Certified Strength and Conditioning Specialist

- Triathlon coach and pre/post natal training instructor

Niki has been sharing her passion for exercise through personal training and coaching for the last 18 years. She truly believes in changing and improving quality of life though fitness. For the last 15 years she has been training at the RDV Sportsplex in Orlando, Florida, a 165,000 square foot state-of-the-art athletic club. Her clientele includes teenagers, expectant moms, competitive triathletes and runners, as well as first time exercisers and seniors. In addition to training, she now manages the fitness staff and loves being surrounded by a passionate team.

Niki has represented the RDV Sportsplex as a fitness expert on local TV "Fitness Tip" spots for Fox 35 News and on local radio shows: The Philips File broadcast on 104.1 FM and Johnny's House broadcast on 106.7 FM.

Niki herself is a competitive age group triathlete, avid runner, yoga instructor, wife and mother of two very active boys!

To contact Niki Davis, check out www.rdvsportsplex.com or directly at: www.ndavis@rdvsportsplex.com
407-916-2543
or loveyourfitness@gmail.com

CHAPTER 16

NUTRITION, EXERCISE & WEIGHT LOSS

BY RICK STREB

Transforming your body doesn't happen by accident. **But it is simple!** The number of calories you eat and the number of calories you burn each day control your body weight. **Calories in vs. Calories out.** So to lose weight, you need to take in fewer calories than you burn. You can do this by becoming more physically active, by eating less, or a combination of both. Your weight loss program should also help you make changes that you can maintain for the rest of your life. **Diets don't work...*lifestyle changes work!!!***

First, and foremost, you should concentrate on employing a healthy meal plan. Consider what you are eating. Unequivocally, nutrition is 70%-80% of the equation necessary to lose body fat.

THE PRINCIPLES OF PROPER NUTRITION

Nutrition is almost always **THE** neglected factor when someone isn't making any progress with their fitness training. And why shouldn't it be? It can be quite confusing.

But understand that without a grasp of proper muscle building and/or fat burning nutrition, you won't be able to make the progress that you desire, and you won't reach your potential.

With a well-implemented nutrition plan, you'll be on your way toward achieving your fitness goals. Why does nutrition seem so confusing? For starters, **there are too many choices**. This makes it very difficult to decide the appropriate course of action.

We have the Hollywood Diet, the Cabbage Diet, the Grapefruit Diet, the Juice Diet, the Zone Diet, high carb, low carb, no carb, high protein, low protein, no protein (okay, maybe not . . . but it wouldn't surprise me), high protein foods, high fat, low fat, SlimFast, Weight Watchers, Jenny Craig, Nutri-System, etc., etc.

Obviously, nutrition is big business!

It can become very frustrating trying to sort through all this information.

I've read thousands of articles, books, and medical journals on nutrition, and I've come to decide on some fundamental principles that all sound nutrition programs do include.

Remember, we are all different, but all essentially the same. **What this means is that the principles of proper nutrition apply to all of us**, but we will need to make certain adjustments for the individual so that you can tailor it to your specific needs, whether it be to build muscle, burn fat, get stronger, or nutrition for your specific sport.

Let's start with a brief introductory look at the three macronutrients – carbohydrates, protein, and fat. All play an important role in your nutrition program. **And YES... there are only three macronutrients!!! Vegetables ARE carbohydrates!**

Carbohydrates – Carbohydrates **ARE** a necessary part of any sound nutrition program. **Carbohydrates are the furnace that fat burns in!** In other words, without sufficient carbohydrates in your meal plan, you will not lose body fat.

Carbs are your muscles preferred energy source for short, intense muscular contractions, i.e., weight training. They supply the energy for these sessions as well as play a crucial role in recuperation and muscle growth.

Ingesting carbs signals your body to release insulin, which transports the amino acids (the building blocks of protein) and the carbs into your muscle cells. This absorption by your muscles is a very important part of the muscle growth and repair factor.

Carbohydrates are stored as glycogen in your body's muscles, and it's this glycogen storage that gives the muscles their fullness.

In addition, **the consumption of carbs creates a "protein sparing" effect**, in that more of your protein will be used for the muscle building process instead of being burned as energy. As you'll see below, **this "protein sparing" is a key element in your nutrition program.**

Some important rules to keep in mind with regard to carbohydrate consumption are…

Avoid all processed foods – This includes: cookies, chips, donuts, pastries, soda, candy – your basic junk food. Processed foods are **"empty"** calories that do nothing for your health or your fitness. By dropping them from your nutrition program, you'll go far in improving your results – building muscle, losing fat, improving sports performance, increasing energy – not to mention vastly improving your health.

Beware! Processed foods can be dressed up in "healthy" packaging. **Read labels.** Stay away from these foods, especially those that contain high fructose corn syrup.

That low fat muffin you're about to eat… put it back. It's loaded with unhealthy sugar. The regular muffin would actually be a better choice.

Get the carbohydrates into your nutrition program from whole grains, fruits, and vegetables.

Protein – Protein, as most of you know, is the building block of muscles. **Without adequate protein consumption, you will be spinning your wheels with regard to your resistance training program.** No nutrition program is complete without proper adequate protein intake.

You should consume a **MINIMUM** of 1 gram of protein per pound of lean body mass every day.

And you may find better results taking in up to 2 grams per day per pound of body weight. At 225 pounds, I've found that roughly 400-450 grams of protein per day works very well for me, which is about 2 grams per pound of body weight.

Fats – Yes, fats. A macronutrient that is more misunderstood than carbohydrates, if that's possible.

Fat is not your enemy. Good or "healthy" fats such as omega 3's and omega 6's are desirable fats.

Here's the problem with most people's nutrition. **They are taking in enough fat but they are taking in the wrong fats by consuming too many trans fatty acids and saturated fats, and not enough good fats.**

Try and eliminate the bad fats (in things such as margarine, shortening, snack foods, and most fast foods).

Consume more of the good fats, such as cold-water fish (salmon), walnuts, ground flax seeds of flax seed oil, hempseed oil, safflower oil, sunflower oil, fish oils, and olive oil.

In addition, taking in enough EFA's (essential fatty acids) is imperative when trying to put on muscle. **Low fat diets suppress the body's ability to produce testosterone, a cardinal sin when trying to build muscle.**

Fats also supply chemical substrates that are necessary for proper hormonal production, as well as protect our vital organs and carry the fat-soluble vitamins to where they are needed.

Fats are an important part of your sports nutrition program to develop muscle, burn fat (yes, burn fat) and get fit and healthy.

Water – Drink it…Drink lots of it…And drink it often.

Seriously, you should be consuming at least 8 – 10 eight ounce glasses of water every day. **Our bodies are made up of 75 percent water.** It's not uncommon for people to dehydrate by 2 percent to 6 percent of their body weight during exercise. The result isn't good. Cell function is disrupted, muscle growth stops, you become mentally and physically sluggish, have a general sense of fatigue and you cannot be on the top of your game.

Sound nutrition includes <u>ALL</u> of the macronutrients. It does not eliminate any of them like most of the "fad" diets do. Keep that in mind the next time you want to start eliminating carbohydrates or fats from your nutrition program.

DIET...THE 4-LETTER WORD

Diet, diet, and diet!

How many times have you heard it?

The answer to a sleek, toned physique is all in the diet.

Well as it turns out, the answers to your questions about how to get and stay in shape are indeed found in the acronym, **D.I.E.T.** It's pretty amazing actually when I looked at the word the other day and suddenly saw all the main components of a successful physique transformation program in the word "diet," right down to the order of importance! Let's take a look:

D: What does the "D" in Diet stand for? The first answer from many people is "Desire." And they're half right. But the correct answer is **"Discipline."**

Everyone has the desire to look great (and be rich, etc., etc.), but for the majority of people that's where it ends. They never do anything about it, they never take any action. And desire without action is simply dreaming.

But a desire to achieve a goal, when combined with consistent action to move toward that goal, becomes discipline. And discipline combined with the next three factors, simply cannot be denied.

In my opinion, discipline, the ability to have faith and stay the course, day after day, no matter what, is the #1 success factor in physique transformation.

I: The "I" is for **"Information"** and is the second most critical facet of a successful physique transformation program. This is where many of those who start their fitness journey quickly lose their way. All the discipline in the world will do you no good if the information you have leads you down the wrong path.

I had a guy walk up to me in the gym recently and he said, "You look great! What do you take? No matter how hard I work, I never change." When I told him the secret was in his diet and not his training, he just looked at me kind of funny and went back to do his next set. His information says he just has to train and take lots of supplements. **His information is wrong!**

You can rest assured that a surgeon, whose skill is often the difference between life and death, did not begin to learn his craft by reading Brain Surgery for Dummies. His skill is the result of the technically sound and proven information he received on the elements required to master a particular skill.

It is so important that you have the right information before you start your physique transformation program. The right information sets a solid foundation for you to build upon, and gives you a thorough, correct grounding in the art and science of physique transformation.

E: The "E" stands for **"Education."** Now with the correct information in hand, this is the process where you actually take the time to understand and learn your craft. And this is where the next group of hopeful aspirants to perfect physiques fall by the wayside. When they realize the physique transformation process requires focus, effort, understanding and time to produce results... they quit. There surely must be an easier way, right?

In physique transformation work, as with most things in life, the path to success is not realized through pills, potions, miracle contraptions or 5-minute a day solutions to lifetime problems. The path to long-term success is always built on the foundation of education.

With little or no education in the art of getting lean, most people result to sheer, brute force. They exercise themselves into oblivion because that's what they think will get them in shape. Invariably, they burn out. Had they taken the time to educate themselves to the task ahead, they would have learned how to accomplish twice as much, with half the effort. That is the essence of education, maximizing results with a minimum of effort.

T: Last in order of importance is 'T' for **"Training."** This is where you actually start to apply the education you have worked so diligently to acquire. In many ways it's the easiest of the four steps. Because expertise is often effortless.

In the gym, the physique transformation expert is often the one that subconsciously pisses people off. First off, she looks great! But she invariably spends much less time on the treadmill or the stationary bike than the ever-present cardio queens, who seem to be permanent attachments to the machines they're on.

In the weight room, he doesn't lift as much weight as the big boys. And he's finishing up his workout while the "hard-core" boys are still on the 20th set of their first body part!

The proper application of knowledge is indeed power! Power to be in complete control of your metabolism… Power to understand how to harness that metabolism to work for you instead of against you… Power to know that you can make dramatic changes to your physique in just a few months' time. . . And make it look near effortless.

So there you have it: **D.I.E.T.** It is the answer, after all.

WHICH IS BETTER: EXERCISE OR NUTRITION?

If you are like most people, then the fad diets and trendy exercises that are splashed across popular magazine covers probably leave you more confused than ever about how to meet your fitness goals. It seems like every week there is a new 'results guaranteed' technique for melting pounds or sculpting muscles.

That is probably why so many of my clients approach me with the age-old question: "Which should I focus on to quickly meet my transformation goals – exercise or nutrition?"

This is a great question…and the answer to it may very well be the catalyst that transforms your physique in a way that you never thought possible.

There are three fundamentals for results-driven exercise…

Exercise Fundamental #1:
SAFETY FIRST – I'm not just talking about the usual "consult with a physician before starting an exercise program" – though you always should. The key to successful exercise, that avoids injury while promoting results, begins with the proper use of equipment and correct body alignment.

Exercise Fundamental #2:
CONSISTENCY COUNTS – The truth is out. If you want amazing results then you have to exercise with amazing consistency. There is just no way around it! Make exercise a habitual part of your daily life and be prepared to feel healthier, more energetic and younger than ever.

Exercise Fundamental #3:
CHALLENGE YOURSELF – Your body is such an advanced organism that it quickly adapts to physical demands. This means that the exercise routine that you have been doing for the past six months no longer results in noticeable results. Use your body's unique ability of adaptation to your advantage by constantly challenging yourself with new and exciting exercise routines.

Now back to the original question… "Which should I focus on to quickly meet my goals – exercise or nutrition?"

The bottom line is that exercise and nutrition work hand-in-hand to produce the results that you are after. Results won't come as a result of intense exercise coupled with a poor diet. And likewise a healthy eater has no way to sculpt their body without the use of exercise! For the fastest most permanent results, eat a healthy diet and exercise consistently.

SAMPLE DIET PROGRAM

8:00 AM	Breakfast	3 oz. Oatmeal 16 oz. water Apple (optional)
10:00 AM	Mid-morning Snack	Banana, Protein Shake or Protein Bar
1:00 PM	Lunch	4-6 oz. of lean meat (Chicken, turkey, fish, lean beef) 4 oz. vegetable 16 oz. water
4:00 PM	Mid-afternoon Snack	Apple, Protein Shake or Protein Bar
6:00 PM	Dinner	4-6 oz. of lean meat (Chicken, turkey, fish, lean beef) 16 oz. water
8:00 PM	Evening	4-6 oz. of lean meat (Chicken, turkey, fish, lean beef) Small Salad 16 oz. water

9 RULES FOR SUCCESSFUL WEIGHT-LOSS

• Eat 5-6 small meals per day, one every 2-3 hours

• Eat one portion of protein and complex carbohydrates with every meal.

• Add fibrous carbohydrates to at least two meals daily.

• A portion of food is approximately the size of your palm of your clenched fist.

• Drink at least 8 glasses of water each day.

• Use Protein Shakes whenever necessary to assure you are consuming the optimal levels of required nutrients.

• Plan your meals in advance and record what you eat.

• Plan your grocery list.

• Once a week give yourself a free day to eat whatever you want.

About Rick

Rick Streb, creator of ProDiets.com, is an innovator in fitness and nutrition. He has been a respected member of the health and fitness industry for close to 30 years. He has established himself as one of the top trainers, nutritionists, and coaches for competitive bodybuilding, fitness and figure athletes in the United States today with NONE ever finishing out of the Top 5 in their competitions.

Rick's keen understanding of how to customize eating plans and training programs for each client has given him a special standing in the health and fitness community. Rick's clients have included professional athletes, television and music celebrities, bodybuilding competitors, and fitness models and beauty pageant contestants throughout the United States who participate in his coaching programs and obtain very successful results.

Rick has also built a tremendously successful boutique training business serving women ages 35-55, helping over 750 ladies look and feel better than they ever thought possible, in the past 3 years.

Along the way, Rick has developed a variety of proprietary systems to build effective fat loss nutrition into his clients' programs to ensure that he could maximize their results—no matter what type of client he is working with at the time.

These days Rick has found his true professional calling – sharing what has worked in his own businesses with other fitness entrepreneurs. He coaches and consults with fitness professionals around the world who want to provide the best for their clients by integrating world-class nutrition programming into their businesses, and helps them generate more clients, more profits and more freedom to enjoy life. You could say he is the "trainer of trainers" when it comes to nutrition.

In 2007, Rick received the Community Leadership Award from the President's Council on Physical Fitness & Sports for his commitment to his clients and passion for helping to improve his community. It is that commitment and passion which distinguishes him from other fitness personalities.

Rick is considered to be one of America's leading fitness professionals with 3 fitness-related degrees, a dietetics degree, and over 27 years of experience as a fitness industry leader and numerous fitness and nutrition-related certifications.

His online programs "ProDiets.com" and "The Extreme Fat Loss Formula" have transformed thousands of bodies just like yours through his health clubs, personal training, online training, phone coaching, magazine articles and books.

You can connect with Rick at:
Rick@ProDiets.com
www.Facebook.com/RickStreb